THE ART OF GREEK COOKING

Greek Gastronomy in 65 Traditional Recipes

AIORA

Compiled by Aris Laskaratos, Theodora Pasachidou and Nikoletta Sarri
Translated by Kyra Stratoudaki
Designed by Michele Traversa – designcube.gr

We would like to thank Jayne Gordon for her assistance and advice.

ISBN: 978-618-5369-76-7

First edition June 2023

AIORA PRESS
11 Mavromichali st.
Athens 10679 - Greece
tel: +30 210 3839000
www.aiorabooks.com

Table of Contents

Soups

Laderá and Pulses

Fish and Shellfish

Meat

Introduction

Greek cooking is an ancient art encompassing not only the flavours and ingredients of the Mediterranean diet but also the heritage. It goes back to the time when Greeks believed its basic elements to be gifts from the gods: cereal from Demeter, olive oil from Athena and wine from Dionysus. These items were not only a source of nourishment, but were also used as offerings in religious rituals.

The word 'gastronomy', meaning the art of cooking, comes from the Ancient Greek word *γαστρονομία* (gastronomía), which can be broken down into the words for stomach and knowledge or law. Greek poet Archestratus of Sicily is thought to be the first person to have used this term; it appears in his poem 'Hedypatheia', a gastronomic guide of the fourth century BCE. In it he lays out the principles of good cooking, and gives advice on where to find the best food in the Greek world.

Two thousand years later, Greek cuisine still follows Archestratus' basic principles: fresh, natural produce used in simple cookery with distinct flavours, free of heavy spices and rich sauces. Using a range of local ingredients, recipes have been passed down the generations and cater for seasonal and regional variations. Along the way, Greek cooking has incorporated the influences of other peoples and cultures of the Mediterranean and beyond.

This book comprises sixty-five much-loved, traditional Greek recipes. These healthy and delicious, nutritional dishes for every day or for special occasions are the perfect introduction to the art of Greek cooking.

THE ART OF GREEK COOKING

Greek Gastronomy in 65 Traditional Recipes

Salads and Mezes

In contrast to Western gastronomy which comprises three consecutive courses, in a traditional Greek meal a salad and a variety of mezes are placed in the centre of the table for all to share. They remain there throughout the meal, even as the main course is eaten.

Mezes are small dishes made from a wide variety of ingredients, either fish, meat, pulses or cheeses. Sometimes an entire meal can be made up of mezes only, especially when accompanied by ouzo or tsipouro.

Salads always form part of the Greek cuisine, traditionally reflecting the season and what is freshly available at that time. Blessed by Greek sun, vegetables are abundant, tasty and fresh, as they get quickly from farm to table thanks to the numerous farmers markets.

Χωριάτικη σαλάτα

Tip
*Other ingredients can also be
added: for example, parsley,
pickled krynthm (rock or sea
samphire), wine vinegar.
Instead of serving with bread,
sprinkle with croutons.*

VEGETARIAN

The Art of Greek Cooking

Horiátiki Saláta

Greek salad

A Greek salad is rich in vitamins and minerals, high in protein, good fats and fibre.

INGREDIENTS

SERVES FOUR

- 1/2KG RED, RIPE, HARD TOMATOES
- 1 CUCUMBER
- 1 GREEN PEPPER
- 1 SMALL ONION
- 1 TBSP CAPERS
- 10 OLIVES (APPROXIMATELY)
- 150G FETA CHEESE
- 4 TBSP OLIVE OIL
- 1/2 TSP DRIED OREGANO
- SALT

PREPARATION

1. Rinse and dry all vegetables well. Chop the tomatoes into medium sized pieces. Peel (optional) the cucumber and slice. Cut the pepper into round slices or long sticks. Finely slice the onion.

2. In a salad bowl, mix the tomatoes, cucumber, pepper, onion and capers. Add salt to taste and mix. Place the feta cheese on top.

3. Drizzle olive oil over the salad, sprinkle with oregano and garnish with olives. Serve with bread. The leftover dressing from the bowl is delicious for dunking bread. It leaves the dish shiny and clean!

Πολίτικη σαλάτα

The salad can be enjoyed immediately, but leaving it for a day in the fridge will enhance the flavour.

VEGAN

The Art of Greek Cooking

Polítiki Saláta

Greek-style coleslaw

Info

This salad comes from Constantinople and its name is derived from the Greek nickname for the city, Polis— literally meaning, the City. Many recipes with origins in Asia Minor arrived in Greece in 1922 with the influx of refugees.

INGREDIENTS

SERVES FOUR

- 300G WHITE CABBAGE
- 2 CARROTS
- 1 RED PEPPER
- 2–3 CELERY STICKS, LEAVES INCLUDED
- 1 TBSP PARSLEY, FINELY CHOPPED
- 1 CLOVE OF GARLIC (OPTIONAL)
- 3 TBSP FRESH LEMON JUICE
- COARSE SEA SALT

FOR SERVING
- 4–5 TBSP OLIVE OIL
- 3 TBSP LEMON JUICE OR WHITE WINE VINEGAR

PREPARATION

1. Grate or finely slice the cabbage. Peel the carrots and thickly grate. Chop the pepper into small pieces, discarding the stalk and seeds. Finely chop the celery and leaves.
2. Put the above ingredients in a bowl covered with water and lemon juice. To enhance the flavour, place in the fridge for an hour.
3. Drain the contents of the bowl, sprinkle with coarse sea salt, add crushed garlic if required and squeeze by hand while mixing. Leave to rest.
4. Drain off the liquid. For serving, pour the olive oil, lemon juice or vinegar over the salad and mix well.

Τζατζίκι

For a milder taste, instead of garlic and olive oil, use garlic-infused oil. Pour 100ml olive oil into a jar with 2 peeled garlic cloves and leave for 2 to 3 days. Add the garlic-flavoured olive oil to the dish to taste.

VEGETARIAN

The Art of Greek Cooking

Tzatzíki

Yoghurt and garlic dip

Info

Tzatziki can be served with bread, pitas, breadsticks or as a dip with carrot and celery sticks. It is perfect with grilled meats and many other dishes.

INGREDIENTS

SERVES SIX

- 500G STRAINED GREEK YOGHURT
- 1 LARGE CUCUMBER
- 2 CLOVES OF GARLIC
- 3 TBSP DILL, FINELY CHOPPED (OPTIONAL)
- 4 TBSP OLIVE OIL
- 1 TBSP WHITE WINE VINEGAR
- SALT

FOR SERVING
- 6 BLACK OLIVES

PREPARATION

1. Rinse the cucumber well and chop off both ends. Grate thickly, unpeeled. Sprinkle with salt and leave in a sieve for approximately 15 minutes. Squeeze out the juices by hand.
2. Empty the yoghurt into a bowl. Crush the garlic and add to the yoghurt. (Garlic can be crushed in a mortar and pestle with some salt to make it smooth). Add the squeezed-out cucumber and mix well.
3. Add the olive oil and vinegar. Add salt to taste, and dill (optional). Mix well.
4. To enhance the flavour, place in the fridge and serve cold. Garnish with black olives.

Μελιτζανοσαλάτα

To enhance the flavour, place the aubergine dip in the fridge for 2–3 hours before serving. Garnish with a couple of olives, sprinkle with parsley and drizzle with olive oil.

VEGAN

Melitzanosaláta

Aubergine dip

Info

Aubergines are rich in minerals such as calcium, potassium and iron. They are also rich in sodium, protein and vitamin A and fibre and are low in calories, containing no fat. Instead they absorb the fat from other foods when digested and therefore help in weight control. Aubergines ranked in the top 10 of 120 vegetables for antioxidant content.

INGREDIENTS

SERVES FOUR

- 3 LARGE GLOBE AUBERGINES
- 1 CLOVE OF GARLIC
- 6 TBSP OLIVE OIL
- 3 TBSP FRESH LEMON JUICE OR VINEGAR
- SALT & PEPPER

PREPARATION

1. Rinse the aubergines well. Chop off the stalks. Pierce with a fork in 3–4 places to cook through.
2. Place on a grill or in a baking dish covered in greaseproof paper. Bake for approx. one hour on a low heat, so that they retain their juices.
3. When soft, cut in half. Scoop the flesh into a bowl with a spoon. Discard the skin.
4. Using a fork, mix the aubergine into a pulp. Leave to cool for 15 minutes. Add the olive oil, vinegar (or lemon juice) and crushed garlic and stir until all the ingredients are blended.
5. Add salt and pepper to taste.

Ταραμοσαλάτα

Stale bread can be used in this recipe. White bread makes taramosalata lighter.

The Art of Greek Cooking

Taramosaláta

Cod roe dip

White fish roe is of higher quality as the red version includes food colourants.

INGREDIENTS

SERVES FOUR

- 120G WHITE SMOKED OR CURED COD ROE
- 180G BREAD (NO CRUST)
- 1 SMALL ONION
- 250ML OLIVE OIL
- 80ML FRESH LEMON JUICE

FOR SERVING

- TOASTED BREAD OR BREADSTICKS

PREPARATION

1. Place the bread in a bowl, cover it with water to let it soften. Before using, drain well.

2. Liquidize the onion in a food processor. Add the fish roe and blend until smooth. Add 1/3 of the bread and blend. Add 1/3 of the oil and keep blending. Repeat until all bread and oil have been used.

3. Add half the lemon juice and blend well. Add the remaining lemon juice. Blend well.

4. Serve with toasted bread or breadsticks.

Τυροκαυτερή

VEGETARIAN

Tirokafterí

Spicy feta cheese dip

Info

In Greece, feta is the most common cheese. It has PDO status (protected denomination of origin) and is made of goat and sheep's milk.

INGREDIENTS

SERVES FOUR

- 250G FETA CHEESE
- 1 SMALL DRIED HOT RED PEPPER
- 1/4 TSP SMOKED PAPRIKA
- 2 TBSP OLIVE OIL
- 2 TBSP VINEGAR
- 1 TBSP WATER

PREPARATION

1. In a food processor, blend the pepper.
2. Add the remaining ingredients and blend until smooth. Empty the contents into a bowl.
3. To enhance the flavour, place in the fridge for at least one hour before serving.

Μπουγιουρντί

Tip

To peel fresh tomatoes easily, score the underside with a cross. Place in boiling water for one minute and then transfer to cold water. With a knife, peel away the skin.

VEGETARIAN

Bouyiourdí

Feta cheese, pepper & tomato bake

Info

The name of this dish, originates from the Turkish word for a written command' or injunction. In the Ottoman Empire, an injunction would be bad news. Today, the word is used to mean a large bill or fine. This is probably as a result of the spiciness of the dish.

INGREDIENTS

SERVES FOUR

- 1 LARGE RIPE TOMATO, PEELED
- 1 LONG GREEN HOT PEPPER, THINLY SLICED (SEEDS INCLUDED)
- 200G FETA CHEESE
- 1 TSP OREGANO
- PINCH OF HOT RED PEPPER FLAKES
- 1 TBSP OLIVE OIL

PREPARATION

1. Preheat the oven to 200ºC.
2. In an ovenproof dish (preferably ceramic), place the block of feta cheese. Layer the tomato, long green pepper and pepper flakes on the cheese.
3. Bake for approximately 15 minutes or until the cheese melts. Sprinkle with oregano, drizzle olive oil and serve.

Στραπατσάδα

Tip

For a richer dish, add 180g of Greek kavourma (a mix of various cured and uncured meats with herbs and spices, shaped like a salami). Sauté the kavourma and add to the tomato sauce. Alternativelly, use cured pork.

Strapatsáda

Scrambled eggs in tomato sauce

Info

The word 'strapatsada' comes from the Italian 'uova strapazzate', meaning scrambled eggs. The dish is also known as 'kayganas', from the Turkish word 'kaygana', which in turn comes from the Persian هنیگاخ [khâgine], meaning omelette. This dish is made all over Greece with minor variations.

INGREDIENTS

SERVES FOUR

• 4 HARD, RIPE TOMATOES
• 6 EGGS
• 2 TBSP EVAPORATED MILK
• 100G FETA CHEESE, GRATED
• 4 TBSP OLIVE OIL
• SALT & PEPPER

FOR SERVING
• FINELY CHOPPED PARSLEY (OPTIONAL)
• TOASTED BREAD

PREPARATION

1. Peel the tomatoes (see *Tip* on p. 26). Chop them into halves or quarters and scoop out seeds.
2. Finely chop the tomatoes, remove most liquid and pour into a frying pan. Cook over a medium heat until the liquid evaporates, approximately 10 minutes. Add the olive oil and stir.
3. In a bowl, beat the eggs. Add the milk, salt and pepper. Add the feta cheese and stir.
4. Pour the beaten eggs over the tomatoes. Stir the mixture and cook for a few minutes over a medium heat. Remove from heat when the egg is cooked. Do not overcook, as the dish can become very dry.
5. Sprinkle with finely chopped parsley and serve with toasted bread.

Φάβα

VEGAN

The Art of Greek Cooking

Fáva

Split peas

The preparation of split peas varies from region to region. In Santorini, they are mixed with caramelized onions to make 'married fava'. Elsewhere, onions are sautéed in olive oil and then poured over the split peas as they are served.

INGREDIENTS

SERVES FOUR

- 500G SPLIT PEAS
- 2 MEDIUM-SIZED ONIONS, THICKLY SLICED
- 1 SPRIG OF THYME
- 5 TBSP OLIVE OIL
- 1.5 LITRES OF WATER
- SALT

FOR SERVING
- OLIVE OIL
- LEMON
- OREGANO
- CAPERS
- ONION OR SPRING ONION

PREPARATION

1. Place the split peas in a bowl and cover in water. Leave for 30 minutes and drain.

2. Heat the olive oil in a large, thick-bottomed saucepan over a medium heat. Sauté the thickly sliced onions and the thyme for 7–8 minutes until soft but not brown. Add the split peas and the water. Bring to the boil and then turn down the heat. Remove the thyme. Simmer for approximately 50 minutes with no lid, skimming off any dark foam from the surface when needed. The peas are ready when they are mushy.

3. Season with salt. Purée the peas in a food processor.

4. Sprinkle with lemon juice, olive oil, oregano and garnish with capers and finely sliced onions or spring onions. Serve warm preferably.

Πιπεριές Φλωρίνης

Tip

Florina peppers can be grilled, but are even better barbequed.

VEGAN

Piperiés Florínis

Sweet red peppers

Info

The peppers and this dish are named after Florina, a town in north-western Greece. The region's cool, dry climate is ideal for growing these sweet, long, red peppers.

INGREDIENTS

SERVES TEN

- 8–10 SWEET LONG RED PEPPERS
- 5 TBSP OLIVE OIL
- 4 TBSP FRESH LEMON JUICE OR WHITE WINE VINEGAR
- SALT

PREPARATION

1. Rinse the peppers well. Cut off the stalk ends and remove the seeds. Dry and place on greaseproof paper in a baking tray.
2. Preheat the oven to 200°C. Bake for 20 minutes on both sides until soft, and either the skins blister or start to go dark.
3. Place in a bowl. Cover and leave for 10–15 minutes, sweating to make peeling easier.
4. Once peeled, chop vertically into 4 strips or cut into round slices. Drizzle over olive oil and lemon juice or vinegar. Sprinkle with salt to taste.
5. To store peppers in the fridge for up to a month, put in a jar and cover with olive oil. Remove from the fridge 15 minutes before serving to bring up to room temperature.

Λιαστές ντομάτες

Choose ripe but firm fleshy tomatoes with few seeds. Alternatively, cherry or baby plum tomatoes can be used.

VEGAN

Liastés Domátes

Sun-dried tomatoes

Info
Traditionally, sun-dried tomatoes are made in August and September, when tomatoes are abundant and ripe. They are dried in the sun, leaving a sweetness and delightful fragrance. Drying 1kg of fresh tomatoes will result in 100g of dried tomatoes.

INGREDIENTS

FOR A 250G JAR

- 16 FRESH PLUM TOMATOES
- 3 CLOVES OF GARLIC
- 4 TSP COARSE SEA SALT
- 1 ROSEMARY SPRIG
- 1 BAY LEAF
- 1 TSP OREGANO

ALSO REQUIRED
- TULLE

FOR STORING
- A STERILIZED JAR
- OLIVE OIL TO COVER THE TOMATOES IN THE JAR

ΣPREPARATION

1. Rinse the tomatoes, cut them in half and discard seeds. Drain for at least 2 hours in a sieve.

2. Cover a roasting tin with greaseproof paper. Place the tomatoes and sprinkle with coarse sea salt (approximately 1/2 tsp over 3–4 pieces of tomato). Place the tin outside in the sun. Cover with tulle to protect from insects, taking care not to touch the tomatoes. At night, take indoors. After 7–8 hours of sunshine for 5 days, they will be sundried tomatoes. Alternatively bake the tomatoes in a preheated oven at 85°C for 3 hours, turning them over once.

3. To preserve, place in sterilized jars. Add the garlic and the herbs and cover in olive oil. If air tight, they can be preserved at room temperature. Once opened, refrigerate.

THE ART OF GREEK COOKING

Greek Gastronomy in 65 Traditional Recipes

Soups

Soups are the most soothing and restorative meal in the Greek cuisine. They are simple recipes, made with a variety of raw ingredients in a single saucepan, and are consumed as a main dish. Soups are usually served in winter. Fasolada soup is considered the national dish of Greece.

Ψαρόσουπα

If the fish is large, cut off the head so that it fits in the pan. Never chop fish into small pieces while it's raw. If you want to be sure the fish is cooked, separate the two filets from the spine, high up near the head. When the flesh is separated easily, the fish is ready.

Psarósoupa

Fish soup

Info

In Greece this delicious fresh fish soup is made with a variety of Mediterranean fish, traditionally, the catch of the day. As fish varieties differ around the world, local fish can be used. Small lobster and crab make the soup even more delicious.

INGREDIENTS

SERVES FOUR

- 1KG FRESH, GUTTED LARGE AND SMALL FISH
- 2 SMALL ONIONS, CHOPPED INTO QUARTERS
- 2 CARROTS, CHOPPED INTO 4
- 2 SMALL FRESH COURGETTES, CHOPPED INTO 4
- 2–3 MEDIUM SIZED POTATOES, CHOPPED IN HALF
- 4 CELERY STICKS
- JUICE OF ONE LEMON
- 3 TBSP OLIVE OIL
- SALT & PEPPER

PREPARATION

1. If not already done, clean the fish of its scales and guts. Rinse well under the tap, especially the inside and the gills. Place the fish in a colander and sprinkle with salt all over it, inside and out.

2. Mix the onions, potatoes, carrots and courgettes and place a layer of the mixture at the bottom of a large saucepan. Place the whole fish on top of the vegetable layer. Add the celery sticks and enough cold water to cover the fish.

3. Bring the soup to the boil. Skim off the froth whenever needed. With lid partly on, from the moment the soup starts to boil, continue to boil on a medium to high heat for 20 minutes. Add salt and pepper and the olive oil. Boil for another 10 minutes with the lid removed.

4. With two spatulas, take the fish out, taking care not to crush. Place in a dish. Keep warm and covered so that the outside does not dry out. Take the vegetables out and put in a bowl. Cover so that they do not dry out. Sieve the liquid, so that any bones or scales are removed.

5. Put the liquid into the saucepan again, adding the boiled vegetables and all fish without the bones. Serve with fresh lemon juice.

Κοτόσουπα

Kotósoupa

Chicken soup with rice

Info

Chicken soup is considered medicinal as it is highly nutritious. It is always served hot and makes an excellent starter.

INGREDIENTS

SERVES EIGHT

- 1 CHICKEN (APPROX. 1.2KG)
- 2 LITRES WATER (APPROX.)
- 1 LARGE CARROT, PEELED, CHOPPED IN HALF
- 100G MEDIUM-GRAIN WHITE RICE
- SALT & PEPPER
- 1 BAY LEAF (OPTIONAL)

FOR THE EGG & LEMON SAUCE
- 40ML FRESH LEMON JUICE
- 1 EGG AT ROOM TEMPERATURE, SEPARATED INTO YOLK AND WHITE

PREPARATION

1. Rinse the chicken and place it in a saucepan with the carrot. Add enough water to cover the chicken. Add the bay leaf (optional). When the water boils, add the salt. Carefully skim off the froth from the surface and discard it. Turn down the heat, partly cover the pot with a lid and let it simmer for 35–45 minutes (depending on the size of the chicken) or until the chicken is cooked.

2. Place the boiled chicken and carrot in a dish and let them cool for 5 minutes. If the liquid in the pan has a lot of fat floating on the surface, remove it with a large spoon or a slice of bread, leaving as little or as much as preferred (See *Tip* p. 40).

3. Sieve the liquid, keeping 300–400 ml in a separate bowl. Add the rice to the remaining liquid, and boil on a medium heat for 15–17 minutes.

4. Discard the skin and bones of the chicken. Chop the meat into pieces small enough to eat with a spoon. Slice up the carrot. Finally, place all these ingredients into the liquid with the rice. Add pepper to taste.

5. **For the egg and lemon sauce:** Beat the egg white in a bowl until almost stiff. Add the yolk and beat in. Take the bowl with the rest of the chicken stock and add the lemon juice. Pour this into the bowl with the beaten egg and stir.

6. Pour the egg and lemon sauce into the saucepan. Combine by moving the saucepan around in a circular motion or stir gently with a spoon.

Γιουβαρλάκια

The Art of Greek Cooking

Yiouvarlákia

Meatball & rice soup with egg & lemon sauce

Info

'Yuvarlak' in Turkish means round.

INGREDIENTS

SERVES SIX

- 800G MINCED BEEF
- 70G MEDIUM-GRAIN WHITE RICE
- 1 EGG
- 50G BUTTER
- 2 MEDIUM SIZED ONIONS
- 25G PARSLEY, FINELY CHOPPED
- 1 TSP OREGANO
- 2 TBSP VINEGAR
- 2 TBSP OLIVE OIL

- 2 LITRES OF WATER
- SALT & PEPPER

FOR THE EGG & LEMON SAUCE
- 250ML JUICE FROM THE SOUP
- 2 EGGS
- 40ML FRESH LEMON JUICE

PREPARATION

1. Put the minced meat in a bowl. Finely chop the onions and add to the mince. Add the parsley, half the amount of rice, the egg, vinegar, olive oil, oregano, salt and pepper. Mix well and place in the fridge for 2 hours.

2. Boil the water in a saucepan. Shape the mince mixture into table tennis-sized balls and drop them one by one into the boiling water. Turn down the heat. Leave to simmer. Add the butter and stir gently.

3. After half an hour, rinse the remaining rice and add to the soup. Boil for 15 minutes. The yiouvarlakia should be firm and not soft, or they will fall apart.

4. **For the egg and lemon sauce:** Beat the egg whites in a bowl until almost stiff. Add the yolks and beat in. Add the lemon juice and keep stirring. Add 1/2 cup of liquid from the yiouvarlakia while still stirring.

5. When the yiouvarlakia are ready, turn off the heat. Pour the sauce over them and gently shake the pan to spread. Leave to set for 10 minutes.

6. Serve the soup hot with ground pepper to taste.

7. If reheating the soup, do so on a very low setting (75°C maximum) so the egg and lemon sauce does not separate.

Τραχανάς

VEGETARIAN

The Art of Greek Cooking

Trachanás

Thick soup made from wheat flour granules

Info

Trachanas is a type of pasta, made from flour, eggs and milk or yoghurt. The pasta is irregularly shaped, fine or coarse, sweet or sour. In some regions of Greece, a sauce made of tomatoes is used when making trachana, giving it a red colour.

INGREDIENTS

SERVES FOUR

- 200G TRACHANAS
- 150G FETA CHEESE ROUGHLY CRUMBLED BY HAND
- 1 TBSP OLIVE OIL OR BUTTER
- 1 LITRE WATER
- SALT

PREPARATION

1. Boil the water in a saucepan.

2. Once boiling, add the olive oil or butter, the trachanas and salt. Keep stirring to avoid any sticking to the pan.

3. As soon as the ingredients start to boil add the feta cheese and keep stirring.

4. After approximately 10–15 minutes, the trachanas will thicken. Remove from the heat. As it cools down, it thickens even more. If the soup becomes too thick simply add boiling water.

Φακές σούπα

Tip

Lentil nutrients are best absorbed when eaten with rice. The amount of protein absorbed by the body is equal to that of red meat. Just add 80g medium grain white rice while boiling the lentils.

The Art of Greek Cooking

Fakés Soúpa

Lentil soup

Info

Known for over eight thousand years, lentils are the most common pulses in the Mediterranean diet, the highest in fibre and rich in iron.

INGREDIENTS

SERVES FOUR

- 300G BROWN LENTILS
- 1 MEDIUM ONION, FINELY CHOPPED
- 1 CLOVE OF GARLIC, FINELY CHOPPED
- 2 TOMATOES, GRATED OR FINELY CHOPPED
- 2 BAY LEAVES
- 1 TSP OREGANO
- 4 TBSP OLIVE OIL
- 2 LITRES WATER
- SALT

FOR SERVING
- VINEGAR (OPTIONAL)

PREPARATION

1. Rinse the lentils and boil in 750ml water for 5 minutes. Drain.
2. In a saucepan, put the rest of the water, lentils, onions, tomatoes, garlic, bay leaves and pepper. Cover the pan.
3. Bring to the boil, then turn down to a medium heat. Cook for 35–45 minutes until the lentils are soft, depending on preference. Add water for a more liquid soup.
4. When ready, turn off the heat, add salt, olive oil and oregano and stir well. When serving, if desired, add 1/2 teaspoon vinegar.

Φασολάδα

VEGAN

Tip

When buying dried beans, avoid any that are yellow or flakey—these are stale and will not boil well even if soaked for hours! If celeriac leaves are hard to find, replaced with celery leaves.

The Art of Greek Cooking

Fasoláda

Bean soup

Info

Fasolada is Greece's national dish. It is highly nutritious as are all pulse dishes.

INGREDIENTS

SERVES FOUR

- 350G DRY BEANS
- 1 MEDIUM ONION
- 2 CARROTS SLICED LENGTHWAYS
- 1 TBSP TOMATO PURÉE
- 2 TBSP CELERIAC LEAVES
- 1 CLOVE OF GARLIC
- 1 LEVEL TSP HOT RED PEPPER FLAKES (OPTIONAL)
- 4 TBSP OLIVE OIL
- SALT & PEPPER

FOR SERVING
- FINELY CHOPPED CELERY

PREPARATION

1. Soak the beans in a large bowl with plenty of water for at least 8 hours before cooking, so that they soften and increase in size.
2. After soaking, put the beans in a large saucepan and cover with plenty of cold water. Bring to the boil. Simmer for 35–40 minutes until parboiled. Remove and drain.
3. Finely chop the onion, celeriac leaves, garlic and carrots. Put 2–3 tbsp of olive oil in a deep saucepan and add the finely chopped vegetables. Stir well on a medium heat for 2–3 minutes. Add the tomato purée and mix.
4. Add the parboiled beans and cover ingredients with 4–5cm of hot water. Put on the lid and simmer for 30–35 minutes. Add salt and pepper to taste and pepper flakes, if required.
5. Finally, towards the end, add the rest of the olive oil. Boil the beans for a few more minutes until soft and the juice looks like a thick sauce.

THE ART OF GREEK COOKING

GREEK COOKING

Greek Gastronomy in 65 Traditional Recipes

Laderá and Pulses

Nature on one plate, a feast of colour and flavour! Laderá are typical dishes of the Greek cuisine. They are based on summer vegetables, herbs and olive oil, and are equally if not more delicious when served one or two days after cooking. Usually, they are accompanied by bread and feta cheese.

Pulses are low in cost but rich in protein and minerals, and have always been a staple in the Greek diet. Butter beans, lentils, split peas, chickpeas and broad beans have been in widespread use for many centuries. They are easy to prepare, wholesome and make for delicious dishes when cooked Greek style!

Τουρλού

VEGAN

Tourloú

Vegetables baked in the oven

Info

This dish name comes from the Turkish 'türlü' meaning 'varied'.

INGREDIENTS

SERVES SIX

- 2 MEDIUM-SIZED AUBERGINES
- 2 COURGETTES
- 1 RED PEPPER
- 1 GREEN PEPPER
- 2 POTATOES
- 2 CARROTS
- 3 RIPE TOMATOES, FINELY CHOPPED
- 2 ONIONS, FINELY COPPED
- 50G PARSLEY, FINELY CHOPPED
- 2 TBSP OREGANO OR FINELY CHOPPED MINT
- 3 CLOVES OF GARLIC
- 100ML OLIVE OIL
- 250ML WATER
- SALT & PEPPER

PREPARATION

1. Rinse the vegetables. Chop the aubergines, courgettes and carrots into large pieces, roughly 3x3cm. Cut the peppers into round slices and the potatoes into cubes of approx. 3x3x3cm. Put everything in a deep baking tray or ceramic dish with a lid.
2. Add the onions. Peel and crash the garlic. Add to the vegetables. Add the tomatoes. Sprinkle with parsley and oregano or mint.
3. Add salt and pepper and pour in the olive oil. Add the 250ml water to cover the base of the baking tray or ceramic dish.
4. Preheat the oven to 200°C. Cover the ceramic dish with the lid (or cover the baking tray with greaseproof paper) and bake for approximately one hour, in a fan-assisted oven. Take the lid off and bake for another 1/2 hour. Check from time to time and add a little water if needed. When ready, tourlou should be dry with only the olive oil remaining.

Ντολμαδάκια

Tip

Mince can be added to the filling. Sauté the onions, add 200g of minced beef and stir well. Add the rice and the remaining ingredients.

VEGAN

Dolmadákia

Vine leaves stuffed with rice

Info

The word 'dolma' is Turkish and comes from the verb 'dolmak', which means 'to be filled'.

INGREDIENTS

SERVES EIGHT

- 70 FRESH AND TENDER VINE LEAVES OR FROM A JAR
- 130G MEDIUM-GRAIN WHITE RICE
- 1 MEDIUM-SIZED ONION, FINELY CHOPPED
- 3–4 SPRING ONIONS, FINELY CHOPPED
- 30G DILL, FINELY CHOPPED
- 3 TBSP MINT OR PARSLEY, FINELY CHOPPED
- 150ML OLIVE OIL
- 60ML FRESH LEMON JUICE
- 500ML WATER
- SALT & PEPPER

PREPARATION

1. If the vine leaves are fresh, rinse them well. Bring a pan of water to the boil. Place the vine leaves in the pan and boil for another 4–5 minutes. Drain thoroughly. If the vine leaves are from a jar, drain well.

2. **For the filling:** Heat half the olive oil and sauté the onions. Add the rice and keep stirring until the rice glistens. Add the lemon juice, herbs, salt and pepper. Keep stirring until the juices are absorbed. Remove from heat.

3. Cover the bottom of a large saucepan with two layers of vine leaves.

4. From the remaining vine leaves, take one leaf at a time with the veins facing upwards. Place a teaspoon of filling in the middle of each leaf and wrap into small rolls, not too tightly. Pack close together in the saucepan, so that they do not unwrap. Put 2–3 layers on top of each other.

5. Pour the remaining olive oil over the dolmades. Add 500ml water. Use an upside-down plate to hold the dolmades in place. Put the lid on the saucepan and let them simmer for 20–30 minutes until the rice is soft and only oil remains in the pan.

Γεμιστά

Tip
Aubergines, courgettes and onions may also be used to make gemista. Pine nuts and raisins may be added to the stuffing.

VEGAN

Gemistá

Stuffed peppers & tomatoes

Info

Gemista is a summer dish, made when tomatoes and peppers are ripe and in season.

INGREDIENTS

SERVES SIX

- 6 RIPE TOMATOES
- 6 GREEN BELL PEPPERS
- 12 LEVEL TBSP OF MEDIUM-GRAIN WHITE RICE
- 1–2 POTATOES, CHOPPED INTO LARGE CHUNKS
- 2 MEDIUM-SIZED ONIONS, FINELY CHOPPED
- 2 CLOVES OF GARLIC, FINELY CHOPPED

- 3 TBSP PARSLEY, FINELY CHOPPED
- 2 TBSP MINT, FINELY CHOPPED
- 1 LEVEL TBSP OF TOMATO PURÉE OR 200G OF FINELY CHOPPED TOMATOES
- 1 TSP SUGAR
- 80ML OLIVE OIL
- SALT & PEPPER

PREPARATION

1. Wash the tomatoes and peppers and dry them. Slice the top off each vegetable to create a lid. Empty the seeds from the peppers and cut away any fleshy parts from the inside. The fleshy parts may be kept, chopped and added to the stuffing mixture but not the seeds. For the tomatoes, once you have sliced a lid, empty the inside with a teaspoon and put the contents in a food processor, blend until liquid.

2. Place the olive oil over medium heat in a saucepan and sauté the onion and garlic for 3–4 minutes. Add the rice, liquified tomato and the purée or finely chopped tomatoes. Add salt and pepper, sugar, parsley and mint. Stir lightly and turn down the heat. Let the rice absorb the tomato juices and partly cook.

3. Preheat the oven to 180ºC. Take the pan off the heat. Let the mixture cool down before stuffing the tomatoes and peppers. Place them upright in a large, deep roasting tin. Put on their lids and drizzle some olive oil over the top. Add more chopped tomato over the top for extra liquid. Add the potatoes around the stuffed vegetables and cook for about 1.5 hrs.

Ιμάμ μπαϊλντί

VEGAN

Instead of roasting the aubergines, fry them. (The dish becomes tastier but also heavier). Pour olive oil into a large frying pan, turn up to a high heat, add the aubergines and fry each side for 3–4 minutes. Place the fried aubergines (slit side down) on plenty of kitchen paper, so that the oil is absorbed.

Imám Bayildí

Roast aubergines

Info

Imam bayildi is a dish with Turkish origins (literally, 'the imam fainted'). Legend has it that an Imam actually fainted because the dish was so tasty. Imam bayildi is found all around the eastern Mediterranean and is called similarly. It is prepared virtually the same way everywhere it is found.

INGREDIENTS

SERVES FIVE

- 10 MEDIUM-SIZED AUBERGINES
- 6 LARGE, RIPE TOMATOES
- 6 MEDIUM-SIZED ONIONS
- 6 CLOVES OF GARLIC
- 3TBSP PARSLEY
- 1 TSP SUGAR
- 180ML OLIVE OIL
- 120ML WATER
- 40ML FRESH LEMON JUICE
- SALT & PEPPER

PREPARATION

1. Rinse the aubergines well. Discard stalks. Score them length-wise. Roast in a pre-heated oven, in 180°C for 40–45 minutes.

2. In the meantime, peel and finely chop the tomatoes. Chop the onions into thin slices and finely chop or crush the garlic. Put these in a bowl, add the tomatoes, finely chopped parsley, salt, sugar and pepper. Mix thoroughly.

3. Remove aubergines from the oven and with a spoon open the middle (not the edges) like a small boat. Place the prepared stuffing into these slits. Pack tightly next to each other in a deep roasting tray. If there is any stuffing left over, pour over them. Pour over the lemon juice, olive oil and 120ml water.

4. Preheat the oven to 200°C. Cover the roasting tin with greaseproof paper and foil, and squeeze tightly around the edges, so there is no gap. Bake for 45–60 minutes until the juices have been absorbed and only the oil remains. Take off the cover and continue baking for another 10 minutes until browned on top.

Φασολάκια

There are many types of green beans, just as there are many types of pans, cookers and personal preferences. In the last 15 minutes of cooking, taste the beans. If soft beans are desired, add small amounts of water, 100ml at a time. When fully cooked, there should be no liquid with the beans.

VEGAN

The Art of Greek Cooking

Fasolákia

Green beans in tomato sauce

Info

Traditionally, this is a summer dish although frozen green beans are available all year. Green beans are a source of vitamins K, C, as well as a- and β-carotene and lutein.

INGREDIENTS

SERVES FOUR

- 1KG FRESH OR 850G FROZEN GREEN BEANS
- 2 POTATOES CHOPPED INTO CUBES
- 2 CARROTS CHOPPED IN ROUND SLICES
- 2 SMALL ONIONS, FINELY CHOPPED
- 250G GRATED OR FINELY CHOPPED TOMATOES
- 25G PARSLEY, ROUGHLY CHOPPED
- 250ML HOT WATER
- 1 TSP SUGAR
- 70ML OLIVE OIL FOR COOKING
- 50ML OLIVE OIL FOR SERVING
- SALT & PEPPER

PREPARATION

1. If using fresh green beans, chop off the ends and remove the long side fibres if necessary.
2. Heat 70ml oil in a large saucepan. Sauté the onions, potatoes and carrots for 3–4 minutes while stirring. Add the sugar.
3. Add the green beans and stir for 1–2 minutes until they are mixed in.
4. Add the tomatoes and water and stir. Once boiling, turn down the heat. Add salt, pepper and the parsley. Stir well and leave to simmer with the lid on. After 15–20 minutes, the beans will be ready, but may be on the crunchy side. If any water remains, turn up the heat and boil with the lid off for a further 10 minutes.
5. Serve at room temperature adding olive oil and ground pepper. This dish is perfect with feta cheese and bread.

Αγκινάρες αλά πολίτα

VEGAN

Aghináres Políta

Lemon artichokes in sautéd vegetables

Info

Artichokes are rich in vitamin B, like B3 (niasin), B1 (thiamine) and folic acid, as well as minerals (e.g. potassium, calcium, phosphorus), vitamin C and vitamin K. Artichokes are good for cholesterol, help lower blood pressure as well as symptoms of irritable bowel.

INGREDIENTS

SERVES FOUR

- 8 PEELED ARTICHOKES
- 7 SPRING ONIONS, FINELY CHOPPED
- 2 MEDIUM-SIZED ONIONS, FINELY CHOPPED
- 2 CARROTS, CHOPPED
- 3 BIG POTATOES, CHOPPED INTO LARGE CHUNKS
- 25G DILL, FINELY CHOPPED
- 3 TBSP PARSLEY, FINELY CHOPPED
- 1 TBSP PLAIN FLOUR
- 80ML FRESH LEMON JUICE
- 100ML OLIVE OIL
- 400ML WATER
- SALT & PEPPER

PREPARATION

1. Heat the olive oil in a wide, shallow saucepan and lightly sauté the finely chopped onion for 3–4 minutes. Add the spring onions, artichokes, carrots and potatoes as well as a tablespoon of plain flour. Sauté for a little longer.
2. Add 400ml boiling water. Put the lid on the saucepan, turn down the heat and simmer for 30 minutes until the artichokes are soft and have absorbed all the liquid apart from the oil.
3. Towards the end, add the dill and parsley. Pour over the fresh lemon juice.

Σπανακόρυζο

VEGAN

Tip

To make a tomato sauce version of this dish, add either some passata, one finely chopped tomato or one tbsp tomato purée to the water and oil mixture. Also, spinach can be substituted for leek or cabbage.

The Art of Greek Cooking

Spanakórizo

Spinach & rice

This dish is highly nutritious. The combination of the ingredients—spinach, rice and lemon—helps with the absorption of nutrients. Spinach is high in B vitamins, which help the immune system and protect the heart.

INGREDIENTS

SERVES FOUR

- 1KG SPINACH, WASHED
- 100G MEDIUM-GRAIN WHITE RICE
- 1 MEDIUM-SIZED ONION, FINELY CHOPPED
- 5-6 SPRING ONIONS, FINELY CHOPPED
- 1 LEEK, FINELY CHOPPED
- 25G DILL, FINELY CHOPPED
- 40ML FRESH LEMON JUICE
- 80ML OLIVE OIL
- 250ML WATER
- SALT & PEPPER

PREPARATION

1. Heat half the oil in a saucepan or a deep frying pan and sauté the spring onions, the onion and leek for 3–4 minutes until soft. Roughly chop the spinach and add to the pan. Continue to sauté for 2–3 minutes until soft.

2. When the spinach has reduced, add the rice and mix well. Add the water to the juices already produced by the vegetables. Add salt and pepper and simmer for 15–20 minutes.

3. When complete, add the remaining olive oil and sprinkle with the dill. Pour in the lemon juice and stir. Cover the pan with a cloth and leave for 5–10 minutes until the juices are absorbed.

4. Serve with extra lemon juice (optional).

Αρακάς

Tip

This dish can also be made with fresh tomatoes. To the peas add 250g of finely chopped tomatoes or fresh tomatoes puréed in a blender.

VEGAN

Arakás

Greek-style peas

Info

Because of their colour, peas are often assumed to be a vegetable. They are in fact a highly nutritious pulse. They are starchy and rich in carbohydrates, fibre, protein, vitamins A, B6, C and K, as well as phosphorus, magnesium, copper and zinc. Peas have a very short growing season, which starts in May and lasts only a few weeks. This is the reason why most of the peas consumed worldwide are frozen.

INGREDIENTS

SERVES FOUR

- 1/2 KG FRESH PEAS, WASHED (OR FROZEN PEAS)
- 2 MEDIUM CARROTS
- 2 MEDIUM POTATOES
- 1 MEDIUM ONION
- 4–5 SPRING ONIONS
- 25G DILL, FINELY CHOPPED
- 80ML OLIVE OIL
- 300ML BOILING WATER
- SALT & PEPPER

PREPARATION

1. Finely chop the onion and spring onions. Slice the carrots and cut the potatoes into small cubes of approx. 2x2x2cm.
2. Heat half the olive oil in a saucepan and sauté the above ingredients.
3. Add the peas, salt and pepper and 300ml boiling water.
4. Cover the saucepan and simmer for 20 minutes. Add the remaining olive oil and finely chopped dill. Take off the lid and boil for 10 minutes on a high heat until the liquid has evaporated.

Γίγαντες

Tip

Pepper can be substituted for hot red pepper flakes.

VEGAN

Gígantes

Butter beans baked in the oven

Info

In Greece, this dish is usually served during Lent. In the Greek Orthodox religion, traditionally, there are seven weeks of fasting before Easter.

INGREDIENTS

SERVES FOUR

- 350G BUTTER BEANS
- 1 LARGE ONION, FINELY CHOPPED
- 2 SMALL CARROTS, FINELY SLICED
- 3 SMALL TOMATOES, FINELY CHOPPED OR LIQUIFIED IN A FOOD PROCESSOR
- 1–2 LARGE TOMATO, FINELY SLICED
- 1 LEVEL TSP SUGAR
- 2 SMALL CLOVES OF GARLIC, FINELY CHOPPED
- 1/3 BUNCH OF PARSLEY, FINELY CHOPPED
- 80ML OLIVE OIL
- 1/2 TSP OREGANO
- SALT & PEPPER

PREPARATION

1. Soak the butter beans in water overnight. The next day, rinse well. Place in a large saucepan with cold water and boil for approximately 40 minutes, until soft. Occasionally, skim off the froth. Discard the water and put the butter beans in a deep roasting tray (approx. 23x33cm) or a ceramic dish.

2. In a deep frying pan, over a medium heat, cook the chopped onion in half of the olive oil until soft. Add the garlic and carrot, and sauté for 2–3 minutes until the ingredients have softened slightly but not browned. Add the sugar, chopped or liquified tomatoes, parsley, salt and pepper. Boil the mixture for 10 minutes and pour on top of the butter beans.

3. Add the remaining olive oil plus approx. 1 cup of water. Cover the beans with the tomato slices to prevent the beans drying out. Cook in a preheated oven at 200°C for about 45 minutes until the juices have evaporated and only the oil remains. Sprinkle with oregano before serving.

Ρεβιθάδα

VEGAN

Revitháda

Chickpeas baked in the oven

Info

Revithada is a traditional dish from Sifnos island, which is cooked in a 'skepastaria'. A skepastaria is a ceramic pot with a fitted lid, produced by local potters specifically for cooking revithada in the oven.

INGREDIENTS

SERVES SIX

- 1/2KG CHICKPEAS
- 2 ONIONS, THICKLY SLICED
- 2 BAY LEAVES
- 100ML OLIVE OIL
- SALT & PEPPER

FOR SERVING

- FRESH LEMON JUICE
- OREGANO

PREPARATION

1. Soak the chickpeas in water for at least 12 hours before cooking. Rinse well and place in an ovenproof lidded dish (approx. 23x33cm), so that the juices do not evaporate.
2. Add the onions, olive oil, bay leaves, salt and pepper and cover the ingredients with water.
3. Put on the lid and place in the oven for about 4 hours at 150°C, until the chickpeas become mushy. Lift the lid from time to time and, if needed, add more hot water so the chickpeas are always covered.
4. Serve revithada with fresh lemon juice and oregano.

THE ART OF GREEK COOKING

Greek Gastronomy in 65 Traditional Recipes

Fish and Shellfish

Greece is very closely linked to the sea: the nation has 6,000 islands and a shoreline of over 15,000 kilometres. Fishing boats, fishers and fish tavernas can be found on every island and in every seaside location. Wooden boatbuilding has always been a large part of local craft, and small wooden fishing boats are typical of Greece's coastal scenery.

Fish have been widely used in Greek cuisine since ancient times. Fresh fish will never fail to impress, the basic rule being that small fish are best fried and larger ones best grilled or barbecued. Shellfish, including molluscs, are plentiful in Greek waters and form the basis of a number of delicious dishes.

Ψάρι πλακί

Tip

Instead of liquifying the tomatoes, they can be sliced and placed on top of the fish. In this case, make the sauce with the rest of the ingredients.

The Art of Greek Cooking

Psári Plakí

Baked fish in tomato sauce

Info

The word 'plakí' probably originates from ancient times when food was cooked on a hot 'plaka' (slab).

INGREDIENTS

SERVES FOUR

- 1KG FISH FILLETS OR A 1KG FISH
- 4 MEDIUM-SIZED POTATOES
- 3 MEDIUM-SIZED ONIONS
- 500G RIPE TOMATOES
- 1 TBSP TOMATO PURÉE
- 100G PARSLEY, FINELY CHOPPED

- 5 CLOVES OF GARLIC
- 2 BAY LEAVES
- 1/2 TSP OREGANO
- 5 TBSP WHITE WINE
- 40ML FRESH LEMON JUICE
- 6 TBSP OLIVE OIL
- SALT & PEPPER

PREPARATION

1. Rinse the fish and dry with kitchen towel. When using one large fish, score it lightly on both sides. Sprinkle with salt, pepper and oregano on both sides.

2. Cut the potatoes into round slices. Oil a deep baking tray and place in the potatoes flat. Sprinkle with salt and pepper. Cut the onions into round slices and place on top of the potatoes.

3. Peel and liquify the tomatoes in a food processor. Empty into a bowl. Meanwhile, stir 2 tablespoons of water into the tomato purée and add to the bowl. Slice the garlic, break the bay leaves by hand and add to the mixture. Finally, add the remaining olive oil, wine and parsley and mix together.

4. Place the fish on top of the sliced onions and pour over the prepared sauce. Preheat the oven to 180°C and bake uncovered for approximately one hour.

5. Baking time will depend on the size of the fillets. Smaller pieces will require less time. For a runnier dish, cover the baking tray and remove cover for the final 20 minutes of baking.

Μπακαλιάρος σκορδαλιά

Tip

Leaching the saltfish may sound easy but can be tricky. The idea is to remove excess salt. Keep in mind that if the fish remains in the water for too long, it may become tasteless and its flesh squishy. Testing is vital—see Preparation.

Bakaliáros Skordaliá

Cod with garlic dip

Info

This dish is traditionally served on 25th March to celebrate the Annunciation and the Greek War of Independence.

INGREDIENTS

SERVES FOUR

FOR THE COD
- 1KG SALTED COD (SALTFISH)
- OIL FOR FRYING

FOR THE BEER BATTER
- 150ML COLD BEER
- 80G PLAIN FLOUR
- 25G CORNFLOUR
- 15G BAKING POWDER
- PINCH OF SALT

FOR THE GARLIC DIP
- 1/2KG POTATOES OR 300G STALE BREAD (NOT CRUST)
- 3–4 CLOVES OF GARLIC
- 40ML FRESH LEMON JUICE OR WHITE WINE VINEGAR
- 6 TBSP OLIVE OIL
- PINCH OF SALT
- 50G CRUSHED WALNUTS (OPTIONAL)

PREPARATION

1. For the cod: Rinse well, chop into big chunks, debone and put in cold water for 1–2 days. The water must be changed every 4–6 hours. After 24 hours, cut a small piece of fish, dip in boiling water for 3–4 minutes and taste it. If still too salty, leave it in the water and taste again after a few hours. When unsalted, take the cod out of the water and dry well.

2. For the batter: Place a metal mixing bowl in the fridge. Half an hour later, mix in this bowl the plain flour, cornflour, baking powder and salt. Pour in the cold beer. With finger tips lightly stir for approx. 1 minute. The batter should be quite runny. Place in the fridge for 20 minutes.

3. Place the cod in a dish, skin side up, placing each piece as far apart as possible. Coat in flour. Dip each piece in batter for a few seconds. Fry in oil over very high heat for 3–4 minutes, until golden. Place on kitchen towel for 4–5 minutes for the oil to be absorbed. Serve with the garlic dip on the side.

4. For the garlic dip: Peel, chop and boil the potatoes in a saucepan of water with salt. When cooked, cool and purée in a food processor until smooth. (If using bread instead of potatoes, soak in water and drain well.) Peel garlic and crush well. Squeeze the lemons and pour juice into the puréed potato or well-drained bread. Add the crushed garlic. Mix well, add the olive oil and keep stirring until all the ingredients are blended. Add the crushed walnuts (optional). Put the garlic dip in the fridge to cool.

Χταπόδι με κοφτό μακαρονάκι

Tip

*Boiling on very low heat
for over an hour is the secret
to this recipe's success.*

Htapódi me Koftó Makaronáki

Octopus with short pasta

Info

Octopus is high in omega-3 fatty acids. It has very low cholesterol, about the same as other fish and almost half that of other seafood. It is an excellent source of vitamin B12, iron, selenium, phosphorus and zinc and has significant amounts of magnesium.

INGREDIENTS

SERVES FOUR

- 1 FRESH OCTOPUS, AROUND 1–1.5KG
- 2 SMALL ONIONS, CHOPPED IN ROUND SLICES
- 2–3 CLOVES OF GARLIC
- 4–5 BAY LEAVES
- 4 TBSP RED WINE
- 2 TBSP OLIVE OIL
- 1 TSP OREGANO

- 500G SHORT PASTA (I.E. RIGATONI, PENNE, FUSILLI)
- 1 TSP SALT
- GROUND PEPPER

FOR SERVING
- 2 TBSP PARSLEY, FINELY CHOPPED

PREPARATION

1. Rinse the octopus well. Separate the tentacles and cut the mantle into 3–4 pieces. Put all the pieces in a saucepan. Add the bay leaves. Put on medium heat with the lid on. There is no need to add water, the juices of the octopus will be released after a short time. Once these juices are boiling, turn down the heat and simmer. After approximately one hour, pour in the wine. Leave to simmer for a further 15–20 minutes until only a thick sauce remains.

2. Remove 5–6 tentacles. These can be chopped into small pieces and served separately with olive oil and either vinegar or lemon juice. Sprinkle with oregano.

3. Chop the remaining octopus (mantle and 2–3 tentacles) into smaller pieces. Leave in the saucepan with the sauce.

4. Boil salted water in a separate saucepan. Add the pasta and boil until ready. Drain.

5. Meanwhile, put 2 tbsp of olive oil in a frying pan, and sauté the onions and garlic for 3–4 minutes. Turn off the heat and add the octopus pieces together with their sauce. Mix well. Add the cooked, drained pasta. Stir to mix the flavours.

6. Serve with ground pepper and finely chopped parsley.

Καλαμάρια γεμιστά

The Art of Greek Cooking

Kalamária Gemistá

Stuffed squid

Info

As with all seafood, squid goes off very quickly. Fresh squid can be kept in a sieve, in the fridge, for one day only. To defrost frozen squid, place in the fridge. Never leave at room temperature.

INGREDIENTS

SERVES FOUR

- 1KG SQUID, CLEANED
- RIPE TOMATOES, LIQUIFIED
- 3 LARGE ONIONS, FINELY CHOPPED
- 3 HEAPED TBSP PARSLEY, FINELY CHOPPED
- 4 HEAPED TBSP DILL, FINELY CHOPPED
- 150G WHITE RICE, RINSED
- 2 TBSP RAISINS
- 180ML WHITE WINE
- 6 TBSP OLIVE OIL
- WATER
- SALT & PEPPER

PREPARATION

1. Finely chop the tentacles. Put half the oil in a large frying pan and sauté the onions until slightly soft. Add the chopped tentacles and stir for a short time until they change colour.

2. Add the raisins, herbs, salt and pepper, the rice and approximately 160ml water. Stir well. Let the rice absorb the liquid, then remove from heat.

3. Stuff the squid with the cooled mixture, leaving room for the rice to increase in volume without causing the squid to tear.

4. In a large saucepan, place the squid in a circle next to each other, so that they fill the bottom of the pan and the stuffing does not spill out. Do not pack too tightly, to allow room for the rice to increase in volume. Pour over the remaining oil, add the wine. Add enough water to cover the squid.

5. Cook on a low heat. Approximately 20 minutes later, add the tomatoes, salt and pepper. Continue cooking until the squid is tender, the rice is cooked, and the sauce is thick. If the squid risks sticking to the bottom of the pan before it is cooked, add more wine.

Μυδοπίλαφο

Tip

Traditionally, mydopilafo is made with medium-grain white rice, but other rice types can be used, such as Arborio.

The Art of Greek Cooking

Midopílafo

Mussels with rice

Info

Of all shell fish, mussels are the lowest in cholesterol. Mussels with rice have a high nutritional value because of the iron, vitamin C, vitamin B-12 and omega-3 fats.

INGREDIENTS

SERVES FOUR

- 1.5KG MUSSELS
- 300G MEDIUM-GRAIN WHITE RICE
- 1 MEDIUM ONION, FINELY CHOPPED
- 200G TOMATOES, FINELY CHOPPED OR GRATED (OPTIONAL)
- 120ML WHITE WINE
- 150ML OLIVE OIL
- 2 LITRES WATER
- SALT & PEPPER

PREPARATION

1. Rinse the mussels thoroughly under running water for 3–4 minutes to get rid of sand and other debris. Scrub shells with a brush or metal scourer. Remove the beard (byssus), by pulling off. Discard any open or broken mussels. Fresh mussels should be tightly closed.

2. In a large saucepan, boil the mussels for 5 minutes until they open. Shake the pan every minute so that they cook evenly but not too much, so that the shells stay intact. Discard any mussels that do not open.

3. Remove with a slotted draining spoon, separate the insides with a knife and place in a dish. Drain and keep the liquid.

4. In a saucepan, sauté the onion in the oil. Add the mussels and stir continuously. Add the wine and 3–4 cups of the withheld liquid. Add salt and pepper. Add the tomato (optional). Leave to boil for 5–10 minutes.

5. Add the rice and simmer with all the ingredients until the rice is cooked and all liquid has been absorbed.

Σουπιές με σπανάκι

Tip

In Crete, when cuttlefish are softened during cooking, their sack is torn, and the ink is emptied out. The dish darkens in colour and is even tastier.

The Art of Greek Cooking

Soupiés me Spanáki

Cuttlefish in spinach

Info

The word 'sepia', used to denote a reddish-brown colour, comes from the Greek word for cuttlefish, 'sipia', which in Latin became 'sepia'. The dark sepia-coloured ink from cuttlefish was used widely in writing from Greco-Roman times until the end of the nineteenth century.

INGREDIENTS

SERVES SIX

- 1KG CUTTLEFISH (FRESH OR FROZEN)
- 1KG FRESH SPINACH, ROUGHLY CHOPPED
- 10 SPRING ONIONS, FINELY CHOPPED
- 50G DILL, FINELY CHOPPED
- 1 TSP OREGANO
- 1/4 TSP CUMIN
- ZEST AND JUICE OF ONE UNWAXED LEMON
- 6 TBSP OLIVE OIL
- SALT & PEPPER

PREPARATION

1. If using frozen cuttlefish, thaw in a sieve over a large bowl. Cover the bowl with a wet cloth or clingfilm and place in the fridge. Cuttlefish is thawed when it is elastic and soft.
2. Rinse the cuttlefish well. Boil some water in a saucepan. Add the cuttlefish and boil for 2–3 minutes. Remove with a slotted spoon and place in a bowl.
3. Cut each cuttlefish in half, separating the sack from the tentacles. Chop the tentacles in half and slice the sack into strips.
4. In a saucepan, heat the oil over a medium to high heat and sauté the spring onions, dill and cuttlefish. When the liquid produced boils, turn down the heat. Leave to simmer for approx. 30 minutes.
5. Add the spinach, oregano, cumin, salt and pepper. Leave to boil for 20 more minutes, until all liquid has evaporated and only the oil remains.
6. Remove from heat. Add the zest and juice of a lemon. Lightly mix with a wooden spoon. Extra lemon juice can be added to taste.

THE ART OF GREEK COOKING

Greek Gastronomy in 65 Traditional Recipes

Meat

Meat consumption in the traditional Greek diet followed the Ancient Greek saying 'pan metron ariston'—'moderation is best'. Meat was thought of as a luxury for Sundays or festive meals.

In Greek cuisine, recipes with meat are mainly based on lamb, goat, pork or chicken, while in recipes with minced meat, beef is most commonly used. In some regions, game dishes are also served.

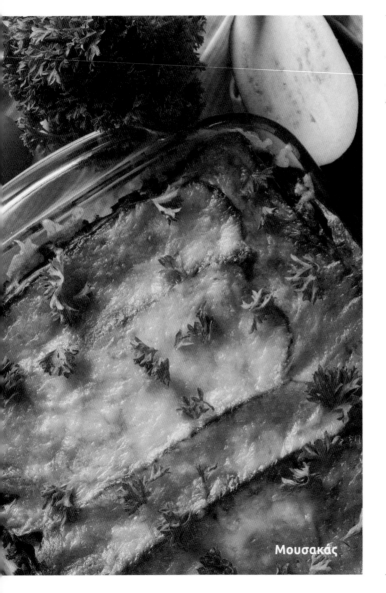

Μουσακάς

Tip

Moussakas is best eaten when the dish is rested for 2 hours before serving. Sprinkle with finely chopped parsley on top.

Moussakás

Aubergines & minced meat with béchamel sauce baked in the oven

Info

Moussakas is a dish served in every Greek restaurant. Created by the famous Greek Chef from Sifnos, Nikolaos Tselementes (1878–1958), his name is a synonym for 'Cook book' in Greek.

INGREDIENTS

SERVES TEN

- 5 LARGE GLOBE AUBERGINES
- 10 MEDIUM SIZED POTATOES
- 5 TBSP OLIVE OIL
- SALT & PEPPER

FOR THE MINCE
- 500G MINCED BEEF
- 500G TOMATO PASSATA
- 1 ONION, FINELY CHOPPED
- 1 CLOVE OF GARLIC, CRUSHED

- 5 TBSP RED WINE
- 1 TSP SUGAR
- 2 TBSP OLIVE OIL
- SALT & PEPPER

FOR THE BÉCHAMEL SAUCE
- 1 LITRE MILK
- 100G BUTTER
- 100G PLAIN FLOUR
- 1/2 TSP GROUND NUTMEG
- SALT & PEPPER

PREPERATION

1. **For the mince:** sauté the onion and garlic in a saucepan with 2 tablespoons of olive oil, until lightly browned. Add the mince and stir frequently until its juices come out. Pour in the wine, add the sugar, passata, 1 teaspoon salt, pinch of pepper and let it boil on a low heat for 25–30 minutes.

2. Peel the potatoes and cut them into slices approximately 1/2cm thick. Put them in a bowl. Add salt, pepper and 2 tablespoons of olive oil. Mix by hand until coated. Lay flat in a large roasting tin and cook for 25–30 minutes at 200°C.

3. Chop the stalks off the aubergines, peel and cut into 1cm slices. Put them in a bowl and add salt, pepper and 3 tablespoons of olive oil. Mix by hand until coated. Put a single layer in a roasting tin and cook for 15–20 minutes at 200°C.

4. **For the béchamel sauce:** place the butter and flour in a saucepan on a medium heat. When the flour is cooked, pour in the milk at room temperature slowly, stirring continuously with a whisk. Add 1 teaspoon salt, a pinch of pepper and 1/2 teaspoon nutmeg. Keep stirring until the mixture is bound together and smooth.

5. In a large roasting tin (approx. 28x38cm), layer the potatoes leaving no gaps. Add a layer of aubergines without leaving gaps. Cover with an even layer of all the mince. Continue layering potatoes, aubergines. Cover the aubergine layer evenly with the béchamel sauce. Cook in the oven at 200°C for 40 minutes until the sauce is golden.

Παστίτσιο

The Art of Greek Cooking

Pastítsio

Pasta & minced meat with béchamel sauce baked in the oven

Info

'Che pasticcio!' when exclaimed by an Italian literally means 'what a mess!' and this sums it up. The term 'pastítsio in literature, art and architecture means something based on previous creations. In the same way, spaghetti-pastítsio is a gastronomic creation made by combining separate yet tasty creations.

INGREDIENTS

SERVES EIGHT

- 1KG MINCED BEEF
- 2–3 MEDIUM-SIZED ONIONS, FINELY CHOPPED
- 400G GRATED TOMATOES
- 3–4 CRUSHED GARLIC CLOVES
- 6 TBSP OLIVE OIL
- 5 TBSP RED WINE
- 70G GRATED KEFALOTIRI (SALTY, HARD, YELLOW, GREEK CHEESE)
- PINCH OF CINNAMON

- 500G THICK, HOLLOW SPAGHETTI
- 1 TBSP BUTTER (FOR GREASING THE TIN)
- SALT & PEPPER

FOR THE BÉCHAMEL SAUCE

- 1 LITRE MILK
- 100G PLAIN FLOUR
- 100G BUTTER
- 1/2 TSP GROUND NUTMEG
- SALT & PEPPER

PREPARATION

1. Pour the olive oil into a deep frying pan on high heat. As soon as the oil is warm, add the chopped onions and sauté until soft (3–4 minutes). Add the mince and stir, breaking it into small pieces with a wooden spoon or spatula. Cook until all the juices have evaporated.

2. Turn down the heat and add the crushed garlic, cinnamon, salt and pepper. Keep stirring for another 3–4 minutes.

3. Add the red wine and 2 minutes later add the grated tomatoes. Mix together and cook for a further 8–10 minutes until almost dry.

4. Boil the spaghetti in a large pan of salty water for 2 minutes less than the time stated on the packet. Drain and empty into a deep roasting tin already greased with butter.

5. Distribute half the spaghetti evenly around the tin. Sprinkle with grated cheese. Add the mince and layer the remaining spaghetti on top.

6. Prepare the béchamel sauce (see p. 89 for preparation) and pour evenly over the top. Optional: add more grated cheese or breadcrumbs to taste.

7. Cook in the middle of the oven at 180–200°C for 50–60 minutes, until golden. Take the tin out of the oven and leave to rest for 30 minutes before serving.

Μελιτζάνες παπουτσάκια

Tip
Instead of using tomato slices to cover the stuffing, béchamel sauce can be used (see p. 89 for preparation).

Melitzánes Papoutsákia

Stuffed baked aubergines

Info

There are many varieties of aubergine in Greece: long, round, purple, white or purple-white. A good aubergine must be smooth, shiny and firm. Papoutsakia in Greek means 'small shoes'.

INGREDIENTS

SERVES FOUR

- 8 SMALL GLOBE AUBERGINES
- 1 LARGE ONION, FINELY CHOPPED
- 300G MINCED BEEF
- 2 CLOVES OF GARLIC, FINELY CHOPPED
- 2 TBSP PARSLEY, FINELY CHOPPED
- 5 MEDIUM-SIZED TOMATOES, FINELY CHOPPED
- 1 TOMATO, SLICED
- 1/2 TSP SUGAR
- 5 TBSP OLIVE OIL
- 40ML WATER
- SALT & PEPPER

PREPARATION

1. Chop the stalk off each aubergine. Wash and cut in half lengthwise. Score deeply and leave in tepid, salty water for 10 minutes to remove bitterness. Dry well. Brush oil into the slits and on the outside. Add salt all over. Put baking paper in a roasting tin and lay the aubergines on it, slit side up. Bake in a preheated fan-assisted oven at 200°C for 20 minutes.

2. Fry the onion, garlic and mince with some salt. Keep stirring until the mince has separated. Put a lid on the frying pan and cook on a low heat for 10 minutes. Add the chopped tomatoes, olive oil, sugar and water, and simmer for 15 minutes. At the end, add salt and pepper to taste, plus the parsley. The stuffing is now ready.

3. Once the aubergines are cooked, press down the flesh with a spoon to create a dent. In that dent, add the stuffing. Pour any liquid left from the mince over each aubergine and cover with 2 slices of tomato. Bake in the oven at 180°C for 45 minutes.

Λαχανοντολμάδες

Tip

*Making lachanodolmades
requires patience and time to
prepare, so it is a dish better
prepared for a lot of people.*

Lachanodolmádes

Stuffed cabbage leaves

Info

Lachanodolmades are traditionally made at Christmas.

INGREDIENTS

SERVES TEN

- 1 LARGE CABBAGE

FOR THE STUFFING
- 750G LOW-FAT MINCED BEEF
- 50G MEDIUM-GRAIN WHITE RICE
- 1 MEDIUM ONION, GRATED
- 4 SPRING ONIONS, FINELY CHOPPED
- 4 TBSP DILL, FINELY CHOPPED

- 2 TBSP PARSLEY, FINELY CHOPPED
- 2 TBSP MINT, FINELY CHOPPED
- 2 TSP SALT
- 1/4 TSP PEPPER
- 4 TBSP OLIVE OIL

FOR THE EGG & LEMON SAUCE
- 2 EGGS
- 40ML FRESH LEMON JUICE
- CORNFLOUR (OPTIONAL)

PREPARATION

1. Clean the cabbage, remove the core, and submerge with the hole from the core pointing downwards, into a large saucepan. Boil for 15–20 minutes, until all leaves are quite soft.

2. In a bowl, mix the onions, finely chopped herbs, mince and rice. Add salt and pepper and half the olive oil. Mix well by hand for 1–2 minutes.

3. Remove the thick veiny middle part of each cabbage leaf, splitting it in two. These half leaves will be stuffed. Depending on the size of each leaf, place approximately a tablespoon full of filling onto each leaf and fold the two sides towards the centre. Roll up from the end to produce a dolma (one stuffed leaf).

4. In a large saucepan, cover the base with a layer of the left over leaves or any not good for stuffing, as well as the veiny middles. Place the dolmades on top of them in a circular fashion, starting from the edge of the pan, moving towards the middle, placing them next to each other so that they will not unwrap. Put another layer on top of the first layer. Add the remaining olive oil and sprinkle with salt and pepper. Place an upside-down plate on the dolmades to hold them in place. Add water to cover the plate, put the lid on and boil. Turn down the heat and simmer for approximately 40 minutes.

5. Using the leftover juice, make an egg and lemon sauce (see p. 43 for preparation). Serve the dolmades with the egg and lemon sauce poured over the top.

Κεφτεδάκια

Tip

Traditionally, keftedakia are fried but alternatively they can be cooked in the oven. Grease a baking tray and cook at 200°C for 20 minutes. Turn over the keftedakia half way through.

The Art of Greek Cooking

Keftedákia

Meatballs

Info

*Dishes with similar names—
such as köfte, kufte, kyufte,
kofta—can be found in India
and Pakistan, the Balkans,
Azerbaijan, Turkey and Iran,
as well as Arabian and North
African countries.*

INGREDIENTS

SERVES FOUR

- 500G MINCED BEEF
- 2–3 SLICES OF STALE BREAD PLUS CRUST, SOAKED IN WATER AND THEN SQUEEZED THOROUGHLY
- 1 EGG
- 2 TBSP FRESH MINT
- 2 TBSP PARSLEY
- 1 TBSP OREGANO
- 3 TBSP WHITE WINE VINEGAR
- 2 MEDIUM SIZED ONIONS, FINELY CHOPPED
- 2 GARLIC CLOVES, FINELY CHOPPED OR CRUSHED (OPTIONAL)
- 2 TBSP OLIVE OIL FOR THE MIXTURE
- SALT & PEPPER

FOR FRYING
- ADDITIONAL OLIVE OIL
- PLAIN FLOUR

PREPARATION

1. In a bowl, combine the mince with all other ingredients and using hands mix well. To enhance the flavour, cover and leave in the fridge for at least an hour. If left overnight, the flavour will be even greater.
2. Put some flour in a shallow plate or on greaseproof paper and shape the mince mixture into small balls, slightly larger than walnut-sized. Flour them and flatten them gently in the middle.
3. Meanwhile in a large frying pan, heat enough olive oil for the keftedakia to be half immersed, and fry for 3 minutes on each side. Once fried, take out and place on kitchen towel to absorb the oil.

Σουτζουκάκια σμυρνέικα

Tip

A dollop of Greek strained yoghurt served on the side is a perfect complement to this dish.

The Art of Greek Cooking

Soutzoukákia Smyrnéika

Meatballs with cumin & tomato sauce

Info

Soutzoukakia originate from Smyrna (modern-day Izmir) in Asia Minor. At the beginning of the twentieth century, immigrants brought soutzoukakia to Greece. The strong taste of cumin is their main characteristic.

INGREDIENTS

SERVES FOUR

- 300G MINCED BEEF
- 200G MINCED PORK OR LAMB
- 1 EGG
- 3 SLICES OF STALE BREAD OR TOAST
- 1 LARGE ONION, GRATED
- 3 GARLIC CLOVES, CRUSHED
- 1/2 TSP GROUND CUMIN
- 1/2 TSP GROUND ALLSPICE
- 1/4 TSP GROUND CINNAMON
- 250ML SWEET RED WINE
- 2 TBSP OLIVE OIL
- SALT & PEPPER

FOR THE SAUCE

- 1KG RIPE TOMATOES, FINELY CHOPPED OR GRATED
- 2 MEDIUM-SIZED ONIONS, FINELY CHOPPED
- 2 CLOVES OF GARLIC, FINELY CHOPPED
- 1/2 TBSP TOMATO PURÉE
- 1/4 TSP GROUND CINNAMON
- 1 PINCH SUGAR
- 4 TBSP OLIVE OIL
- SALT & PEPPER

PREPARATION

1. Soak the bread in the wine, drain and thoroughly mix all ingredients until combined. For enhanced flavour, leave in the fridge for at least one hour.

2. Roll the mince into cylinders (approx. 7–8cm in length and 3cm diameter). Coat in flour and lightly fry in heated oil.

3. **For the sauce:** Heat the oil in a saucepan and sauté the onion and garlic. Add the remaining ingredients and boil for 10–15 minutes until thickened.

4. Place the soutzoukakia in an ovenproof dish (or deep roasting tin). Pour over the sauce and cook in the middle of the oven at 200°C for approximately 25 minutes until browned.

5. Serve with rice, chips, mashed potatoes or pasta.

Σπετσοφάι

Tip

Spetsofai is best served at room temperature and tastes even better the next day.

The Art of Greek Cooking

Spetsofái

Country-style sausages with tomatoes & peppers

Info

This is a summer dish because it is made with ripe vegetables. A traditional recipe from Mount Pelion, its name probably stems from the Italian word speziato, which means spicy.

INGREDIENTS

SERVES FOUR

- 2 LARGE COUNTRY-STYLE SAUSAGES (APPROX. 600G)
- 5–6 LONG PEPPERS, RED AND GREEN
- 2 RIPE TOMATOES
- 1 TSP SUGAR
- 1 MEDIUM-SIZED ONION
- 2 CLOVES OF GARLIC, SLICED
- 2 TBSP OLIVE OIL (OPTIONAL)
- SALT & PEPPER
- PINCH OF HOT RED PEPPER FLAKES (OPTIONAL)

PREPARATION

1. Chop the sausage into round slices and sauté in a large frying pan. Do not use olive oil if they have sufficient fat.
2. Discard the seeds and stalks of the peppers and chop into pieces. Slice the onion into rounds. Add peppers and onions to the sausage. Stir and sauté until the vegetables soften.
3. Peel the tomatoes and finely chop. Add the tomatoes, garlic, salt and sugar to the frying pan.
4. Turn down the heat and let the ingredients simmer until the tomato juice has evaporated. For a spicy dish, add hot red pepper flakes.
5. When almost ready, add plenty of ground pepper. Serve with fresh bread and feta cheese.

Χοιρινό πρασοσέλινο

Feta cheese can also be used in this recipe. Grate 150g of feta and add to the pan before pouring in the lemon sauce. For a thicker sauce, add cornflour.

Hirinó Prasosélino

Pork with leeks & celeriac

Info

Hirino Prasoselino is a winter dish. In northern Greece, in the regions of Macedonia and Thrace, it is traditionally cooked for Christmas.

INGREDIENTS

SERVES FOUR

- 1KG PORK SHOULDER OR NECK, CUT INTO CHUNKS
- 2 LARGE WHOLE CELERIAC
- 2 LARGE LEEKS
- 8 SPRING ONIONS
- 1 SMALL ONION
- 4 TBSP OLIVE OIL
- SALT & PEPPER

FOR THE EGG & LEMON SAUCE
- 1 EGG
- 20ML FRESH LEMON JUICE

PREPARATION

1. Clean the celeriac and place in plenty of boiling water for 2–3 minutes. Drain well, keeping the water for later. Clean the leeks, spring onions and onion and chop into round slices.

2. In a large saucepan, heat half the olive oil and sauté the meat lightly on all sides. Take out the meat with a slotted draining spoon.

3. Add the rest of the olive oil to the pan. Add the celeriac, chopped into slices, and the leeks and onions, and sauté until the vegetables soften. Return the meat to the saucepan and add 2 cups of the water from the celeriac. Add salt and pepper and simmer for an hour and a quarter, depending on the tenderness of the meat.

4. **For the egg and lemon sauce**: Beat the egg in a bowl. Gradually add the lemon juice. Add one cup of the meat juice slowly. Beat the mixture continually so the egg does not cook. Pour the lemon sauce over the meat in the saucepan and swirl in a circular motion so the sauce spreads.

5. Turn off the heat and leave for 30 minutes to allow the sauce to thicken.

Αρνάκι φρικασέ

Tip

For a lighter dish with less fat, replace lamb with goat or kid. Equally, for a lighter egg and lemon sauce, use just the yolks. In a bowl, beat the yolks with 1 teaspoon cornflour diluted in 40ml of water, then add the lemon juice.

Arnáki Fricassée

Lamb stew with egg & lemon sauce

Info

Fricassée is a French word describing a cooking method in which white meat (chicken, rabbit or lamb) is chopped into pieces, sautéed in butter or oil, boiled with vegetables and then served in a white sauce.

INGREDIENTS

- 1.5 KG LAMB CHOPPED INTO PIECES
- 4 LARGE LETTUCES
- 1 LARGE ONION
- 10 SPRING ONIONS
- 50G DILL, FINELY CHOPPED
- 25G PARSLEY, FINELY CHOPPED
- 1 TBSP PLAIN FLOUR
- 4 TBSP OLIVE OIL
- SALT & PEPPER

SERVES SIX

FOR THE EGG & LEMON SAUCE
- 1.5 CUP JUICE FROM THE STEW
- 2 EGGS
- 60ML FRESH LEMON JUICE

PREPARATION

1. Heat the olive oil in a saucepan. Coat the meat with salt and pepper, then coat with flour and sear all sides. Add enough water to partly cover the meat, cover with a lid and leave it to simmer for at least 1 hour, until the lamb is soft.
2. Grate the onion. Chop the spring onions, finely chop the dill and parsley and dry all on kitchen towel.
3. Roughly chop all the lettuce and put in boiling water for 2 minutes. Drain.
4. Sauté the onions, add to the pan with the meat (which is almost cooked). Add all the vegetables.
5. Add salt and pepper and boil for a few minutes. The greens should be tender. Remove from the heat.
6. **For the egg and lemon sauce**: Whisk the eggs in a deep bowl until fluffy. Stir continually while slowly pouring in the lemon juice. Take some liquid from the stew and add gradually, until the temperature of the sauce is the same as the main dish.
7. Pour the sauce over the meat and quickly swirl the saucepan until the sauce is thick and combined.

Κατσίκι στη λαδόκολλα

For a delicious twist, sprinkle with freshly squeezed lemon juice when unwrapping.

The Art of Greek Cooking

Katsíki sti Ladókola

Goat in a pouch

Info

Goats are abundant in Greece, especially on the islands, where they feed on shrubs and wild greens. Goat or kid meat is leaner than lamb while equally tasty.

INGREDIENTS

SERVES SIX

- 1.5KG LEG OF GOAT
- 2 CLOVES OF GARLIC, FINELY SLICED
- 2 CLOVES OF GARLIC, CRUSHED
- 10 ROSEMARY SPRIGS AND EXTRA ROSEMARY LEAVES
- 5 THYME SPRIGS
- 1.5KG NEW POTATOES
- 6 TBSP OLIVE OIL
- COARSE SEA SALT & PEPPER

ALSO REQUIRED
- STRING

PREPARATION

1. With a sharp pointed knife, cut slits in the meat all the way around and insert garlic slices and rosemary leaves. Rub with olive oil all over. Sprinkle with coarse sea salt and pepper.
2. Peel the potatoes (optional).
3. Place 4 long strips of greaseproof paper on a kitchen surface in the shape of a star. Spread onto it the crushed garlic, rosemary and thyme sprigs. Place the meat over the herbs, and the potatoes around the meat. Pour over the remaining olive oil.
4. Lift the greaseproof paper, matching opposite edges. Using the string, tie tightly in the shape of a pouch. There should be no gaps between the paper strips.
5. Place the pouch in a deep roasting tray. Bake in a preheated, fan-assisted oven at 170°C for at least 2.5 hours.
6. Remove from the oven and let it rest for 20 minutes before unwrapping. The meat will be tender and fall off the bone. Serve hot.

Κόκορας κρασάτος

Tip

Before cooking, remove the cockerel from the fridge for at least 30–45 minutes until it reaches room temperature. Before sautéing the meat, dry well with kitchen paper.

Kókoras Krasátos

Cockerel in red wine with pasta

Info

Although considered a classic French recipe (coq au vin), this dish is closely linked with Greek village life.

INGREDIENTS

SERVES SIX

- 1.5KG COCKEREL CUT INTO SIX PORTIONS
- 500G THICK PASTA
- 1 LARGE ONION, FINELY CHOPPED
- 2 RIPE TOMATOES, PEELED AND FINELY CHOPPED
- 2 TBSP OF TOMATO PURÉE
- 4–5 ALLSPICE GRAINS
- 250ML RED WINE
- 5 TBSP OLIVE OIL
- HOT WATER
- SALT & PEPPER
- 100G GRATED KEFALOTIRI CHEESE (OPTIONAL)

PREPARATION

1. Pour the olive oil into a large saucepan and heat on a high temperature. Rub the cockerel pieces with salt and pepper and sauté in the oil until golden.
2. Add the onion and sauté until soft and transparent.
3. Pour in the wine and cook until the liquid is reduced by half. Add the tomato purée, allspice grains and additional salt and pepper.
4. Add the tomatoes and hot water until the meat is almost completely covered. Put on the lid and simmer until the meat falls off the bone. The sauce should be thick and caramelized.
5. Meanwhile, boil the pasta. Drain and drizzle with olive oil until all pasta is covered.
6. Put the pasta in a deep dish, and then place the cockerel pieces on top with the sauce. Grated cheese can be added.

Λαγός στιφάδο

Tip
Although this stew is ideal with hare, rabbit or chicken can be used instead.

Lagós Stifádo

Hare stew with onions

Info

Hare stew is a classic winter dish, traditionally found in mountainous regions.

INGREDIENTS

SERVES EIGHT

- 2KG HARE CUT INTO 8 PIECES

FOR THE MARINADE
- 1 ONION, CUT INTO LARGE CHUNKS
- 6 CLOVES OF GARLIC
- 8 BAY LEAVES
- 500ML RED WINE
- 200ML VINEGAR
- 3 TBSP OLIVE OIL

FOR COOKING THE HARE
- 1.5KG SMALL ONIONS, PEELED
- 2 ONIONS, FINELY CHOPPED
- 1 CARROT, FINELY CHOPPED

- 4 CLOVES OF GARLIC
- 4 ALLSPICE GRAINS
- 6 BAY LEAVES
- 1 CINNAMON STICK
- 4 TBSP OLIVE OIL
- 250ML RED WINE
- 500ML WATER
- SALT & PEPPER

PREPARATION

1. Place the hare pieces into a bowl. Mix the dry ingredients of the marinade in another bowl and add the wine, vinegar and oil. Pour the marinade over the meat and leave in the fridge for 12 hours.

2. Once marinated, the marinade can be discarded. In a large saucepan, heat the olive oil on a medium heat and add the and add the finely chopped onions, the small whole onions, carrot, garlic cloves and spices (bay leaves, allspice and cinnamon). After about 10 minutes, when the vegetables are softer, turn up the heat and add the pieces of hare. Mix for 3–4 minutes until the meat is seared.

3. Add the wine to the saucepan, boil for a minute and then add 500ml water, salt and pepper. Turn down the heat to the minimum setting and simmer for an hour or until the meat is falling off the bone. Stir occasionally, taking care not to crush the small onions. Add boiling water if needed.

Μοσχάρι γιουβέτσι

Tip

For this dish, the best-tasting cuts of veal are the cheek or oxtail.

The Art of Greek Cooking

Moschári Yiouvétsi

Veal & orzo casserole

Info

The name of this dish comes from the clay pot (yiouvetsi) in which it is cooked. This is a deep clay pot with a well-fitting lid. A ceramic or pyrex dish can be used instead, as long as it has a lid.

INGREDIENTS

SERVES SIX

- 1.2KG VEAL CUT INTO SIX PORTIONS
- 750G TOMATO, FINELY CHOPPED OR GRATED
- 1 TBSP TOMATO PURÉE
- 1 CARROT
- 1 SMALL ONION
- 3 CLOVES OF GARLIC
- 2 SPRIGS OF PARSLEY, FINELY CHOPPED
- 1 PINCH SUGAR
- 1 BAY LEAF
- 3–4 ALLSPICE GRAINS

- 5 TBSP RED WINE
- 3 TBSP OLIVE OIL
- 1 LITRE BOILING WATER
- SALT & PEPPER

FOR THE ORZO
- 500G THICK ORZO
- 1.3 LITRES BOILING WATER
- 3 TBSP OLIVE OIL

FOR SERVIMG
- 100–200G GRATED KEFALOTIRI CHEESE (OPTIONAL)

PREPARATION

1. Heat the olive oil in a saucepan and sauté the meat on all sides (3–4 minutes). Add the onion and carrot (whole, unchopped), the parsley and garlic and stir until coated with oil. Add the tomato purée and stir for one minute.

2. Pour in the wine and add the sugar. Add the chopped or grated tomatoes and the water. Add the bay leaf and allspice. Put on the lid and simmer for approximately 1 hour, until the meat is soft. Towards the end, add salt and pepper.

3. Place a ceramic or pyrex dish in the oven and preheat to 200°C. When hot, put the contents of the saucepan into the dish. Add the orzo, olive oil and boiling water. Stir well and cook at 200°C for 15 minutes.

4. Remove the yiouvetsi from the oven, stir and sprinkle with cheese if desired. Put back in the oven for 4–5 minutes. Remove and allow to rest for 10–15 minutes. The juices will be absorbed as the dish cools. Grated kefalotiri cheese can be added.

Σουβλάκι με πίτα

The Art of Greek Cooking

Souvláki me Píta

Greek pita wrap

Info

Souvlaki is an ancient food that was passed down from the Greeks to the Romans to the Byzantines. The Ottomans continued it and it is found all around the eastern Mediterranean and the Middle East. Athenaeus of Naucratis, in Deipnosophists (c. third century CE), his fifteen-volume work on dining customs, writes of a meal called 'kandavlos', which was lamb or goat meat on the spit, very similar to souvlaki.

INGREDIENTS

SERVES FOUR

- 4 PITAS (GREEK, CYPRIOT OR ARAB PITAS CAN BE USED)
- 400G PORK NECK
- 1–2 TOMATOES CUT IN HALF AND THEN SLICED
- 1 MEDIUM-SIZED ONION CUT IN HALF AND FINELY SLICED
- 1 TBSP PARSLEY, ROUGHLY CHOPPED
- 1/2 TSP OREGANO, PLUS A LITTLE EXTRA FOR THE MEAT AND PITA
- SALT & PEPPER
- 4 SKEWERS
- PAPRIKA, SWEET OR SPICY (OPTIONAL)
- THICK YOGHURT, TZATZIKI OR MUSTARD (OPTIONAL)

PREPARATION

1. In a bowl mix together the onion, parsley, oregano, salt and some paprika (optional).
2. Chop the meat into cubes of approximately 2x2x2cm. Push 8–9 cubes of meat onto each skewer.
3. Barbecuing or cooking over charcoal is preferable. Otherwise, use a griddle on medium to high heat. Once hot, cook 2–3 souvlaki skewers at a time. Turn them over and cook well for 2–3 minutes on each side. Turn the heat down, sprinkle with salt and oregano, cover with a lid and cook for another 3–4 minutes until the meat is cooked but not dry. Cook on all sides.
4. In the same griddle, heat the pitas for 2–3 minutes on each side, sprinkling with a tiny amount of salt and some oregano.
5. Lay the pitas flat on the counter, take the meat from the skewer and put in the pita. Add 3–4 slices of tomato plus 1/4 of the onion mix. Add 1–2 tsp yoghurt, tzatziki (see p. 19 for tzatziki recipe) or mustard (optional). Wrap each pita tightly with greaseproof paper, so that it is easier to hold.

THE ART OF GREEK COOKING

Greek Gastronomy in 65 Traditional Recipes

Pies

Wheat, being the basic ingredient of pies, has always been a staple in the Greek diet. Excavations around Greece have revealed wheat seeds from the Neolithic era. In the Iliad, Homer depicts ploughing and harvesting on Achilles' shield. According to mythology, Demeter, the goddess of wheat and cereals, showed humankind how to cultivate the land.

A piece of pie is a piece of Greek gastronomy at its best. Handmade Greek filo pastry is an art in itself, requiring experience and patience. In the old days, girls inherited from their mothers or grandmothers a plastero—a flat, round wooden bat on which to roll out filo pastry. Pies are found all around Greece, in different shapes and forms.

Τυρόπιτα

Tip

The filling can be made with a mixture of cheeses, for example 700g of feta plus 300g of graviera, kefalotiri or mizithra or any yellow cheese desired.

VEGETARIAN

Tirópita

Cheese pie

Info

An ancient dish! In the fifth century BCE, Greek poet Philoxenus of Cythera mentions being served 'a milk-and-honey-made cheesebread and a fine-flour platterbread'.

INGREDIENTS

MAKES TWELVE PORTIONS

• 6 FILO PASTRY SHEETS (SEE P. 129)

FOR THE FILLING

• 1KG FETA CHEESE, ROUGHLY CRUMBLED
• 4 EGGS
• 200G SHEEP'S MILK YOGHURT
• 4 TBSP MILK
• A PINCH OF SALT
• PEPPER (OPTIONAL)

EXTRA

• 6 TBSP OLIVE OIL FOR BRUSHING THE FILO SHEETS

PREPARATION

1. Roughly crumble the feta cheese into a bowl. In a different bowl, beat the eggs and mix in the remaining ingredients, as well as the feta. Add a pinch of salt and if desired a pinch of pepper. Place in the fridge for 15 minutes.

2. Oil a deep baking tray and place the first filo sheet on the base. Do not stretch it. Brush with oil. Repeat with 2 more sheets.

3. The filo sheets should be larger than the baking tray. Empty the filling mixture onto the third sheet. Spread the filling evenly. Cover the filling with the remaining 3 filo sheets, brushing oil on each one before adding the next. Do not cut the filo pastry to size. Brush oil on the top layer of filo. Roll all the layers of overhanging pastry together around the edge of the tray.

4. Sprinkle with water. Score lightly into portions with a sharp knife. Cook near the bottom of a preheated oven at 180ºC for approximately one hour.

Σπανακόπιτα

Tip

Spanakopita can be made with a mixture of spinach and wild greens. This makes for a very tasty variation. For a vegan version, omit cheese or eggs.

Spanakópita

Spinach pie

Info

Spanakopita is considered to be the epitome of Greek pies. Made in all regions of Greece, it is the most traditional of pies and is well known all over the world.

INGREDIENTS

MAKES TWELVE PORTIONS

- 6 FILO PASTRY SHEETS (SEE P. 129)

FOR THE FILLING
- 1KG SPINACH
- 2 LARGE LEEKS
- 4 SPRING ONIONS
- 1 ONION
- 25G DILL
- 25G PARSLEY
- 25G MINT
- 2 EGGS, BEATEN
- 200–300G FETA CHEESE, ROUGHLY CRUMBLED
- 3–4 TBSP PLAIN FLOUR
- 4 TBSP OLIVE OIL
- SALT

EXTRA
- 6 TBSP OLIVE OIL FOR BRUSHING THE FILO SHEETS

PREPARATION

1. Rinse, dry and finely chop the spinach. Finely chop all other vegetables and herbs.

2. Place chopped vegetables and herbs in a large bowl, sprinkle with salt and mix by hand, squashing them. Leave in a sieve for 5 minutes for juices to drain. Squeeze by hand to extract as much liquid as possible. Discard the liquid and put the mix of ingredients back in the bowl. Add the olive oil, eggs, feta, flour and salt. Mix well.

3. Oil a deep baking tray and place the first filo sheet on the base. Do not stretch it. Brush with oil. Repeat with 2 more sheets. The filo sheets should be larger than the baking tray. Empty the filling mixture onto the third sheet. Spread the filling evenly.

4. Cover the filling with the remaining 3 filo sheets, brushing oil on each one before adding the next. Do not cut the filo pastry to size. Brush oil on the top layer of filo. Roll all the layers of overhanging pastry together around the edge of the tin.

5. Sprinkle with water. Score lightly into portions with a sharp knife. Cook near the bottom of a preheated oven at 180°C for approximately one hour.

Κρεατόπιτα

Kreatópita

Meat pie

Info

In the old days, families in many regions of Greece would raise a pig every year and slaughter it just before Christmas. Various parts of the pig would be stored and some meat would be kept for special festive meals. One of those was the New Year's Day meat pie.

INGREDIENTS

MAKES TWELVE PORTIONS

- 6 FILO PASTRY SHEETS (SEE P. 129)

FOR THE FILLING

- 1KG MEAT (CAN BE BEEF, PORK, LAMB OR SHEEP), CHOPPED SMALL OR MINCED
- 4 EGGS, BEATEN
- 5 SMALL LEEKS (OR 2 LARGE ONES), CUT IN ROUND SLICES
- 2 ONIONS, FINELY SLICED
- 2 TBSP PARSLEY, FINELY CHOPPED (OPTIONAL)
- 4 TBSP OLIVE OIL
- 120ML WATER
- SALT & PEPPER

EXTRA

- 6 TBSP OLIVE OIL FOR BRUSHING THE FILO SHEETS

PREPARATION

1. In a large shallow saucepan, heat the olive oil. Sauté the meat or minced meat for 6–7 minutes until browned.

2. Add the leeks and onions. Leave on a medium heat for a few minutes until softened. Stir frequently. Do not let them go brown. Add salt and pepper. Add 120ml water and simmer until dry. Remove from heat. Beat the eggs and add to the meat while stirring. Add parsley if desired. Mix well.

3. Oil a deep baking tray and place the first filo sheet on the base. Do not stretch it. Brush with oil. Repeat with 2 more sheets. The filo sheets should be larger than the baking tray. Empty the filling mixture onto the third sheet. Spread the filling evenly.

4. Cover the filling with the remaining 3 filo sheets, brushing oil on each one before adding the next. Do not cut the filo pastry to size. Brush oil on the top layer of filo. Roll all the layers of overhanging pastry together around the edge of the tin.

5. Sprinkle with water. Score lightly into portions with a sharp knife. Cook near the bottom of a preheated oven at 180°C for approximately one hour. The pie is ready when golden and comes off the tray whole.

Μπατζίνα

Tip

The pumpkin can be replaced with butternut squash or courgettes.

VEGETARIAN

Batzína

Crustless courgette pie

Info

Traditionally from Thessaly in central Greece, batzina is quick and easy to make, requiring no pastry. It is often served cold as a snack.

INGREDIENTS

MAKES TWELVE PORTIONS

- 750G PLAIN FLOUR
- 1KG PUMPKIN
- 2 SMALL LEEKS, FINELY CHOPPED
- 4–5 SPRING ONIONS, FINELY CHOPPED
- 1 MEDIUM-SIZED ONION, FINELY CHOPPED
- 2 EGGS
- 2 TBSP BUTTER
- 500G FETA CHEESE, ROUGHLY CRUMBLED
- 250ML MILK
- 250ML WATER
- 150ML OLIVE OIL
- SALT & PEPPER

PREPARATION

1. Cut the pumpkin in half lengthwise and discard the seeds. Peel and coarsely grate into a sieve. Sprinkle with salt and mix. Set aside for 15 minutes. Squeeze by hand to remove the liquid.

2. Place the grated pumpkin into a bowl. Add the onion, leeks, spring onions and crumbled feta cheese. Add pepper and a little salt, as the feta is already salty.

3. In a separate large bowl, whisk the eggs, milk, water and olive oil. Add 700g of plain flour, keeping the remaining 50g aside.

4. Stir well. If the mix looks very stiff, add some water. Pour this mixture into the pumpkin mixture and using a spoon, stir well.

5. Oil a deep baking tray (approx. 42cm diameter) and dust plain flour over it. Pour the batzina mixture into the tray and spread evenly. Sprinkle the surface with any leftover flour. Lightly push some small blobs of butter into the batzina.

6. Cook near the bottom of a preheated oven at 180°–200°C for approximately 50 minutes. Batzina is ready when golden and comes off the sides of the tray.

Κολοκυθόπιτα

Best served with sprinkled icing sugar and cinnamon.

VEGETARIAN

The Art of Greek Cooking

Kolokithópita

Sweet pumpkin pie

Info

Pumpkins are low on fat yet high in potassium, vitamins A,C, B3 and B1, α- and β-carotene. They have antioxidant and antimicrobial properties and support the immune system.

INGREDIENTS

MAKES TWELVE PORTIONS

- 6 FILO PASTRY SHEETS (SEE P. 129)

FOR THE FILLING
- 1 PUMPKIN (APPROX. 1KG)
- 1 LITRE MILK
- 2 EGGS
- 1 TBSP BUTTER

- 200G SUGAR
- 5 TBSP PLAIN FLOUR
- 100G WALNUTS, ROUGHLY CHOPPED
- 100G RAISINS (OPTIONAL)

EXTRA
- 6 TBSP OLIVE OIL FOR BRUSHING THE FILO SHEETS

PREPARATION

1. Mix the plain flour into 250ml of room-temperature milk, ensuring there are no lumps.

2. In a small saucepan, warm the remaining milk over a low heat. Add the flour and milk mixture and stir. Add the sugar. When thick and creamy, remove from the heat. Beat the eggs separately and add them in. Add the butter and stir continuously until it melts. Leave to cool down. Peel the pumpkin. Chop into pieces approximately the size of table tennis balls.

3. In a separate saucepan, boil the pumpkin until soft. Discard the water and pulp the pumpkin. Mix the pumpkin pulp with the creamy mixture. Add the walnuts and raisins if desired. Mix well.

4. Oil a deep baking tray and place the first filo sheet on the base. Do not stretch it. Brush with oil. Repeat with 2 more sheets. The filo sheets should be larger than the baking tray. Pour in the filling and spread evenly. Cover the filling with the remaining 3 filo sheets, brushing oil on each one before adding the next. Do not cut the filo pastry to size. Brush oil on the top layer of filo. Roll all the layers of overhanging pastry together around the edge of the tray.

5. Sprinkle with water. Score lightly into portions with a sharp knife. Cook near the bottom of a preheated oven at 180°C for approximately one hour, until golden on top and cooked underneath.

Φύλλο πίτας

Fílo Pítas

Filo pastry for pies

Info

The traditional Greek rolling pin is a wooden stick 2–3cm in diameter and 80cm long, called a plastis.

INGREDIENTS

FOR THE FILO PASTRY
- 750G PLAIN FLOUR
- 1 TBSP VINEGAR
- 4 TBSP OLIVE OIL
- 340ML TEPID WATER
- 1.5 TSP SALT

EXTRA FOR ROLLING OUT
- 120G CORNSTARCH OR PLAIN FLOUR

MAKES 6 FILO SHEETS FOR A DEEP ROUND BAKING TRAY OF APPROX. 42CM DIAMETER

PREPARATION

1. Put the flour in a large bowl. Make a well in the centre and add into it the salt, vinegar and olive oil. Mix well. Add the water and mix until the dough comes off the sides of the bowl.

2. Shape the dough into a sphere, place it on a flat surface and knead, until it is smooth, supple and fluffy. If sticky, sprinkle with extra flour.

3. Divide dough into 6. Knead separately for 1 minute and shape into 6 small balls. Sprinkle with flour into the now empty bowl and place in it the 6 small dough balls. Dust with more flour. Cover with a clean cloth and leave to rest for approximately one hour.

4. **Rolling out filo pastry:** On a clean surface, roll out each dough ball into a circular shape, approx. 15–20cm diameter. Dust with flour or cornstarch as required to prevent the pastry from sticking to the surface. Stack on top of each other sprinkling flour or cornstarch between each.

5. Turn the pile upside down and roll out each sheet individually turning each one frequently to shape it into a circular filo sheet. Each filo sheet should be approx. 10cm larger than the baking tray. If rolled with a traditional rolling stick, let the filo wrap around the stick and keep rolling until the required thinness of filo is achieved. If the filo sticks, sprinkle with cornstarch or flour. Repeat for all 6 filo sheets.

THE ART OF GREEK COOKING

GREEK COOKING

Greek Gastronomy in 65 Traditional Recipes

Desserts and Coffee

'Spoon desserts', 'baked desserts', 'syrupy desserts'. Some of these are linked to specific religious events, with kourabiedes and melomakarona consumed at Christmas and halvas during Lent. Syrupy desserts carry influences from the East, mainly from the Turks and the Arabs.

Honey is one of the most used ingredients in Greek desserts, together with nuts, fruit and spices. It is rich in vitamins, minerals and amino acids and is also a symbol of fertility and well-being. Greek honey is considered of the highest quality.

Chocolate is absent from traditional Greek desserts although nowadays it is frequently incorporated into various sweet recipes.

Γλυκό του κουταλιού σταφύλι

Tip

The dessert is ready when a single drop of its syrup will set. To check, place a plate at an angle and drip onto it a drop of syrup. If it sets, the dessert is ready.

The Art of Greek Cooking

Glikó Koutalioú Stafíli

Grape 'spoon dessert'

Info

Traditionally, 'spoon desserts' were made to preserve the flavour and nutrients of fruit for a whole year. Families frequently owned a plain or intricate set of crystal plates passed down the generations. They were tiny, specifically made for serving the dessert with a teaspoon on the side. A variety of fruit can be used to make spoon desserts, such as cherries, sour cherries, figs, oranges and bergamots.

INGREDIENTS

FOR THREE JARS OF 250G

- 1KG YELLOW SEEDLESS GRAPES
- 500G SUGAR
- 1 TSP VANILLA EXTRACT
- 160ML WATER
- 200GR ROASTED ALMONDS (OPTIONAL)
- 2–3 ROSE GERANIUM LEAVES (OPTIONAL)

PREPARATION

1. Rinse the grapes well. Separate them and discard the stems.

2. In a saucepan over a low heat, put the sugar, water and vanilla.

3. When the syrup starts to boil, add the grapes. Occasionally gently shake the pan. Do not stir with a spoon or the grapes will disintegrate. Skim off foam if necessary. Simmer for approximately 10 minutes. Remove from heat to prevent shrivelling.

4. Place a cloth over the pan and cover with a lid. Leave aside for 12–24 hours.

5. The following day bring back to the boil for approximately half an hour.

6. Shortly before removing from the heat, add lemon juice. This acts as a preservative and antiseptic and prevents sugar crystalization. As an optional extra, add almonds and rose geranium leaves.

7. Pour the dessert into warm, sterilized glass jars. Tighten the lid and turn upside down until cold. Store in a cool, dark place.

Χαλβάς

VEGAN

The Art of Greek Cooking

Halvás

Sweet semolina with cinnamon & nuts

Info

Like many traditional Greek desserts, halvas is vegan, as it does not contain any animal-derived ingredients. The word comes from the Arabic word 'hulw' meaning 'sweet'.

INGREDIENTS   SERVES SIX

- 200G COARSE SEMOLINA
- 250G SUGAR
- 6 TBSP OLIVE OIL
- 500ML WATER
- 2 CINNAMON STICKS
- 2 TSP GROUND CINNAMON
- PEEL OF ONE UNWAXED LEMON
- PEEL OF ONE UNWAXED ORANGE
- 100G ALMONDS OR WALNUTS, FINELY CHOPPED
- 75G RAISINS (OPTIONAL)

PREPARATION

1. Put the water, sugar, cinnamon sticks, lemon and orange peels in a small saucepan. The lemon and orange peel is not chopped as it is removed later. Stir over a low heat until the sugar has dissolved. Boil for 5 minutes. Remove from the heat and leave to one side. The syrup is ready.

2. Heat the olive oil in a large saucepan over a medium heat. Do not burn. Add the semolina and stir with a wooden spoon for approximately 6–8 minutes, until it is a dark, golden colour. Add the walnuts or almonds and, if desired, the raisins. Stir well.

3. Remove the saucepan with the semolina from the heat. Add the warm syrup gradually. Take care because the mixture is very hot and can splash easily. Keep stirring, paying particular attention to the edges and base of the pan. This is because semolina turns bitter if it burns. Place the saucepan back on a low heat and stir until the semolina increases in volume, sticks to the spoon and comes away from the side of the pan.

4. Remove the cinnamon sticks and the orange and lemon peels.

5. While the halvas is still warm, pour it into a cake or bread tin. Press down and smooth the surface with a spatula. Leave to cool for 30 minutes. Cover with a serving dish, and holding both the tin and the dish, turn upside down and lift off the tin. Sprinkle with ground cinnamon.

Καρυδόπιτα

VEGETARIAN

Karidópita

Walnut cake

Info

The word for walnut in Greek, is 'carydi'. It comes from the name of a princess in Greek mythology, Carya, whom Dionysus transformed into a walnut tree. Artemis ordered Carya's father to build a temple with his daughter's figure carved into wooden walnut columns. This is how the first Caryatides were made!

INGREDIENTS

SERVES TWELVE

- 7 EGGS
- 200G BUTTER
- 150G SUGAR
- 350G WALNUTS, ROUGHLY CHOPPED
- 150G BREADCRUMBS
- 5 TBSP COGNAC
- 20G BAKING POWDER
- 1 TSP GROUND CLOVES
- 1 TSP GROUND NUTMEG
- 2 TSP GROUND CINNAMON
- ZEST OF ONE UNWAXED ORANGE

FOR THE SYRUP
- 400G SUGAR
- 500ML WATER
- 1/2 TSP VANILLA EXTRACT
- 1 TBSP FRESH LEMON JUICE

PREPARATION

1. In a bowl, mix the walnuts, breadcrumbs, cinnamon, cloves, nutmeg and baking powder.
2. Beat the butter and sugar for 6–7 minutes in a food processor, until smooth. Add the yolks one by one, keeping the whites separate. Add the orange zest and cognac and mix into the dry ingredients.
3. Whisk the egg whites until they form stiff peaks. Fold 3 tablespoons of this into the cake mixture. With a spatula, fold in the remaining whisked egg whites.
4. Grease a cake tin (approx. 23x33cm) and pour in the cake mix. Bake in the middle of a preheated fan-assisted oven at 170ºC for 35 minutes.
5. In a saucepan, place all the ingredients for the syrup. Stir until the sugar has melted and boil for 3 minutes. Set aside to cool.
6. Remove the walnut cake from the oven and score into portions. Pour the cooled syrup over the hot cake slowly so that it is absorbed evenly.
7. Once cold, cover the cake tin firmly with cling film and turn upside down onto the kitchen counter. This will further even out the syrup.
8. As with all syrupy desserts, for enhanced flavour serve after 12 hours.

Ρεβανί

VEGETARIAN

Revaní

Semolina sponge cake with syrup

Info

This dessert is baked all over Greece and the Mediterranean and is called by various different names. It probably originated in Turkey.

INGREDIENTS

SERVES TWELVE

FOR THE REVANI

- 340G COARSE SEMOLINA
- 125G PLAIN FLOUR
- 200G STRAINED YOGHURT
- 4 LARGE EGGS
- 180G SUGAR
- 250ML SUNFLOWER OIL
- 1/2 TSP VANILLA EXTRACT
- 1 TBSP ZEST OF UNWAXED LEMON
- 1.5 TSP BAKING POWDER
- 80G SLICED ALMONDS, PISTACHIOS OR DESICCATED COCONUT (OPTIONAL)

FOR THE SYRUP

- 800G SUGAR
- 750ML WATER
- PEEL OF ONE UNWAXED LEMON

PREPARATION

1. Beat the sugar and sunflower oil in a food processor until smooth. With the blender at medium speed add the yoghurt and then the eggs, one by one, and the vanilla and lemon zest.

2. Place semolina in a mixing bowl and sieve into this the plain flour and baking powder. Stir with a spoon until mixed well. Pour this into the egg and yoghurt mix and blend gently.

3. Oil and flour a baking tin (approx. 23x33cm). Pour in the mix. Spread evenly. Bake in a preheated oven at 180°C for 45 minutes.

4. Meanwhile, place all the syrup ingredients in a saucepan and boil over a medium heat for 3 minutes. Set aside to cool.

5. Once baked, remove the revani from the oven, score lightly into portions and pour over the syrup, one spoonful at a time.

6. Leave to stand for at least 4 hours before serving. Decorate with sliced almonds, pistachios or desiccated coconut (optional).

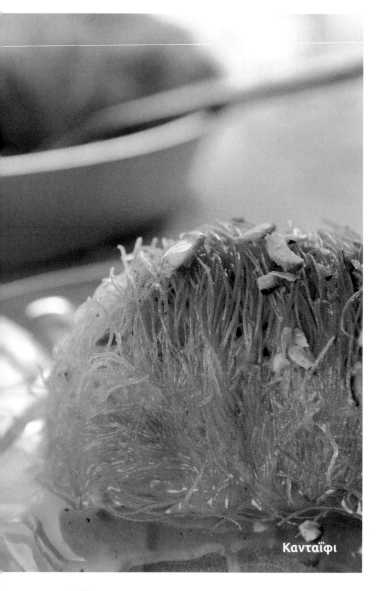

Κανταΐφι

Serve with vanilla ice cream or whipped cream for a unique dessert. Walnuts can be substituted for almonds or pistachios according to preference.

VEGETARIAN

The Art of Greek Cooking

Kadaífi

Walnut in kadaifi shredded pastry

Info

Kadaifi was brought to Greece by migrants from Asia Minor in 1922. A variation of kadaifi, as with most syrupy baked desserts, exists in all eastern Mediterranean and North African cuisines. Depending on the region, kadaifi is served with coffee, tsipouro or raki.

INGREDIENTS

SERVES TWELVE

- 500G KADAIFI SHREDDED PASTRY
- 250G BUTTER
- 3 TBSP SUGAR
- 300G WALNUTS, ROUGHLY CHOPPED
- 2 TBSP BREADCRUMBS
- 1 TSP CINNAMON

FOR THE SYRUP
- 600G SUGAR
- 500ML WATER
- 1 TBSP FRESH LEMON JUICE

FOR TOPPING
- 30G WALNUTS, FINELY CHOPPED

PREPARATION

1. In a small saucepan, melt the butter over a low heat.
2. On a clean surface, open and lay out the kadaifi shredded pastry. Roughly separate the shreds by hand. Keep back 2–3 tablespoons of melted butter. Pour the rest of the butter slowly and evenly covering all the shredded pastry.
3. Grease a shallow baking tin (approx. 23x33cm). Place a layer of half the shredded pastry in the bottom.
4. In a bowl, mix the roughly chopped walnuts, sugar, cinnamon and breadcrumbs. Spread evenly onto the shredded pastry.
5. Add the remaining buttered shredded pastry to cover all the ingredients. Pour over evenly the remaining melted butter.
6. Bake in a preheated oven at 170°C for approximately 45 minutes until the kadaifi pastry is golden.
7. In a saucepan place all the syrup ingredients. Stir until the sugar melts and boil for 3 minutes. Set aside to cool.
8. Once baked, remove the kadaifi from the oven. Pour the syrup slowly and evenly over the hot kadaifi until absorbed. Set aside to cool. Sprinkle with walnuts and serve cold.

Μπακλαβάς

Tip

For a vegan version, olive oil can be used instead of butter.

VEGETARIAN

The Art of Greek Cooking

Baklavás

Nut & filo pastry dessert

Baklava is one of many syrupy desserts common in Greek and East Mediterranean cuisine. Traditionally, different nuts were used depending on local availability. For example, in mountainous regions walnuts were used and elsewhere, pistachios or almonds.

INGREDIENTS

SERVES EIGHTEEN

- 450G READY-MADE FILO PASTRY SHEETS
- 250G BUTTER
- 3 TBSP SUGAR
- 500G WALNUTS, ALMONDS OR PISTACHIOS
- 1 HEAPED TSP GROUND CINNAMON
- 1 LEVEL TSP GROUND CLOVES
- 1 PINCH GROUND NUTMEG

- 18 WHOLE CLOVES
- ZEST OF ONE UNWAXED ORANGE

FOR THE SYRUP
- 2 TBSP HONEY
- 600G SUGAR
- 500ML WATER
- 1 CINNAMON STICK
- 1.5 TBSP LEMON JUICE
- PEEL OF HALF AN UNWAXED LEMON

PREPARATION

1. In a small saucepan melt the butter over a low heat.
2. Grind the nuts in a food processor so they are evenly but not finely chopped. Mix in the sugar, ground cinnamon, ground cloves, ground nutmeg and zest of one unwaxed orange.
3. Brush butter on the bottom and sides of a deep baking tray (approx. 23x33cm). Layer the tray with half the filo pastry sheets, lightly brushing melted butter on each sheet before adding the next. Spread the chopped nuts evenly on top and then layer the remaining filo pastry sheets, lightly brushing melted butter on each sheet.
4. With a sharp knife, cut the excess pastry from the sides of the tray. Score the baklavas into 18 portions, taking care not to damage the pastry sheets. Cut to approximately half way in depth, but do not go through to the very bottom. Press a clove into each portion. Pour over the remaining butter and sprinkle the top with water.
5. Bake near the bottom of a preheated oven at 170ºC for one and a half hours, until golden. Leave to cool for at least 2 hours before pouring onto it the syrup.
6. In a small saucepan, heat all the syrup ingredients. Boil for 3 minutes. Remove the syrup from the heat. Discard the lemon peel and cinnamon stick. Pour over the baklavas, ensuring even distribution. Leave to stand until all the syrup has been absorbed.

Γαλακτομπούρεκο

VEGETARIAN

The Art of Greek Cooking

Galaktoboúreko

Semolina custard pie

Galaktoboureko comes from the words 'gala', meaning 'milk' in Greek, and 'boureki'. In Turkish, 'börek' means 'filo-wrapped pie'.

INGREDIENTS

SERVES TWELVE

- 400G READY-MADE FILO PASTRY SHEETS
- 120G FINE SEMOLINA
- 1 LITRE MILK
- 250G BUTTER
- 4 EGGS
- 180G SUGAR
- ZEST OF ONE UNWAXED LEMON
- 1/2 TSP VANILLA EXTRACT

FOR THE SYRUP
- 400G SUGAR
- 250ML WATER
- PEEL OF ONE UNWAXED LEMON

PREPARATION

1. In a saucepan bring the milk to the boil. Add the semolina, stirring continuously. Remove from the heat when thick and creamy.

2. Beat the eggs with the lemon zest, vanilla and sugar.

3. Put the semolina and milk mixture back on a low heat and slowly add into it the egg mix. Keep stirring for 3–4 minutes. Do not boil. Add half the butter, stir in and leave to cool.

4. Melt the remaining butter. Grease the bottom and sides of a deep baking tray (approx. 23x33cm). Layer the base of the tray with 2/3 of the filo pastry sheets, brushing each one with melted butter. Pour in the cream mixture. Fold in the overhanging filo sheets. Layer the remaining filo sheets on top, brushing butter between each sheet.

5. Pour the remaining butter over the galaktoboureko and score into wide strips. Sprinkle with 2 tablespoons of water. Bake in a preheated oven at 180°C for approx. 45 minutes. Set aside to cool.

6. Put the syrup ingredients (water, sugar, lemon peel) in a saucepan. Boil for approx. 10 minutes. Remove the syrup from the heat. Discard the lemon peel. Pour the hot syrup over the galaktoboureko. Set aside until cold before cutting into portions.

Μελομακάρονα

Tip

No need to grease a baking tin or add greaseproof paper. The oil within the melomakarona prevents them from sticking.

VEGAN

Melomakárona

Cinnamon & honey sweets

Info

Melomakarona are much loved Christmas sweets. They are easy to make and can be stored for several weeks.

INGREDIENTS

MAKES APPROX. TWENTY

- 350ML OLIVE OIL
- 500–600G PLAIN FLOUR
- 10G BAKING POWDER
- 1 TBSP SUGAR
- 1/2 TBSP HONEY
- 3 TBSP COGNAC
- 120ML ORANGE JUICE
- 1 TBSP ORANGE ZEST
- 125G WALNUTS, ROUGHLY CHOPPED
- 1/2 TSP GROUND CINNAMON
- 1/4 TSP GROUND CLOVES

FOR THE SYRUP
- 180G HONEY
- 60G SUGAR
- 80ML WATER

FOR TOPPING
- 30G WALNUTS, FINELY CHOPPED

PREPARATION

1. In a bowl, mix the walnuts with the cinnamon.
2. In a food processor, on slow speed, beat the olive oil until light in colour. Add the honey, sugar and orange zest and continue to beat. The longer this mixture is beaten, the more crunchy and light the sweets will be, also helping to absorb the syrup better.
3. Stir into a cup the cognac, orange juice and baking powder until disolved. Add to the oil and sugar mixture. Add the flour in stages and continue to mix.
4. Knead until the ingredients are bound together, soft and form a ball. (Do not overmix as this results in dense melomakarona). Take a walnut-sized portion of the dough mix and place in one hand. Flatten it and place some of the walnut and cinnamon mix into the middle. Fold the dough over in a long or round shaped pouch depending on preference. Place, seam side down, on a baking tray.
5. Bake in a preheated oven at 175–180ºC for approx. 20 minutes. Set aside to cool.
6. Meanwhile, prepare the syrup. In a large saucepan over medium heat stir the honey, sugar and water. If necessary skim off any froth. Dunk into the syrup 10–12 melomakarona at a time. Leave for approximately 2 minutes. Remove with a flat slotted draining spoon and place on greaseproof paper for the syrup to settle. Move to a shallow serving dish and sprinkle with finely chopped walnuts.

Κουραμπιέδες

VEGETARIAN

The Art of Greek Cooking

Kourabiédes

Butter biscuits topped with sugar

Info

Much-loved traditional Christmas biscuits. The kourabies (singular: kourabies, plural: kourabiedes) originates from Persia (present-day Iran), where it first appeared in the seventh century. It is also very popular in Turkey, the Middle East and the Balkan countries.

INGREDIENTS

MAKES APPROX. FIFTY

- 800G PLAIN FLOUR
- 450G BUTTER AT ROOM TEMPERATURE
- 250G ICING SUGAR
- 2 TBSP COGNAC
- 1 TSP VANILLA EXTRACT

PREPARATION

1. In a food processor beat the butter with half the sugar until smooth and fluffy. Add the cognac and vanilla. Add flour in stages until the dough is firm.

2. Knead lightly the dough and place in the fridge for at least an hour.

3. To ensure all kourabiedes bake evenly, shape dough into similar-sized biscuits, depending on preference. Half-moons and spheres are two traditional shapes.

4. Place on a baking tin leaving some space in between, so that they do not stick together whilst cooking. No need to grease the baking tin.

5. Bake in a preheated oven at 150–160ºC for approximately 40 minutes until golden. Remove. Leave to cool. Sift the remaining powdered sugar over the kourabiedes before they are completely cold.

Ρυζόγαλο

For vegan rizogalo, use non-dairy milk.

VEGETARIAN

Rizógalo

Greek rice pudding

Info

Variations on rice pudding exist all around the world. The dessert is thought to have originated in Asia where the first written record of it appears in two of India's greatest epics, the Mahabharata and Ramayana. In Europe, a precursor of the dish was used by the Romans as a medicine for stomach disorders, and there are recipes for rice pudding dating from the Middle Ages.

INGREDIENTS

SERVES SIX

- 150G ARBORIO OR MEDIUM-GRAIN WHITE RICE
- 1.2 LITRES MILK
- 2 HEAPED TBSP CORNFLOUR
- 100G SUGAR
- 1/4 TSP MASTIC POWDER
- 1 TSP CINNAMON
- 1 PINCH OF SALT
- 600ML WATER

PREPARATION

1. Rinse and drain the rice.
2. In a saucepan, boil 500ml water. Add the salt. Add the rice and simmer over very low heat for 12 minutes.
3. Add the milk, sugar, mastic powder and stir. Dilute the cornflour in 100ml cold water and pour into the saucepan while stirring. Simmer until the mixture thickens.
4. Remove from heat. Divide into 6 small bowls and leave to cool down. When cold, place in fridge.
5. Sprinkle with cinnamon and serve cold.

Ελληνικός & Φραπέ

How to order a Greek coffee or Frappé depending on how much sugar is required:

Sketo [σκέτο]: without sugar

Metrio [μέτριο]: medium, with 1 teaspoon of sugar.

Gliko [γλυκό]: sweet, with 2 teaspoons of sugar.

Ellinikós & Frappé

Greek coffee & instant iced coffee

Info

Greek coffee: *A traditional briki, the Greek coffee pot, is made of copper and is conical in shape. This allows for the even distribution of heat and for best quality foam at the top.*

Instant iced coffee: *Frappé is French for 'beaten'. This type of coffee was invented by chance in Thessaloniki in 1957 by someone who wanted an instant coffee but had no hot water. By beating the ingredients in a shaker, the most popular summer iced coffee was born!*

INGREDIENTS

GREEK COFFEE

- 1.5 TSP GREEK COFFEE
- 1 SMALL CUP OF WATER APPROX. 60ML
- SUGAR: NONE FOR UNSWEETENED COFFEE, 1 TSP FOR MEDIUM SWEET OR 2 TSP FOR SWEET COFFEE

INSTANT ICED COFFEE

- 2 TSP INSTANT COFFEE
- 30ML WATER AT ROOM TEMPERATURE
- SUGAR: NONE FOR UNSWEETENED COFFEE, 1 TSP FOR MEDIUM SWEET OR 2 TSP FOR SWEET COFFEE
- 2 TBSP EVAPORATED MILK OR 4–5 TBSP FRESH MILK (OPTIONAL)
- 3–4 LARGE ICE CUBES
- ICED WATER

PREPARATION

Greek coffee: Pour the water into a briki coffee pot. Place the briki on low heat. Add the coffee and sugar (if required). Stir very well until the coffee is dissolved. Stir frequently until thick foam and bubbles appear on the edge of the pot.

When foam covers the entire surface, the coffee will increase in volume. Remove from heat before it boils. Empty it slowly into a small cup.

Frappé: Place the sugar, coffee and 30ml water in a large glass (250ml). Whisk for a few seconds or beat in a cocktail shaker until everything is dissolved. A creamy foam will form.

Add 3–4 large ice cubes. Pour in the milk according to preference. Top up with iced water until the foam reaches the top of the glass. Drink with a straw.

Tip

When drinking in company, toast Greek-style: 'Yia mas', 'cheers to our good health'!

The Art of Greek Cooking

Drinks

Wine, ouzo, tsipouro, raki & liqueurs

---

*A meal with no wine,
a day with no sunshine.*

Greek proverb

In Ancient Greek mythology, Dionysus, son of Zeus and Semele, was the god of vine and wine. He taught King Oeneus how to cultivate vines in return for the hospitality he received. To honour him, every year in ancient Athens a large festival called Dionysia took place.

Today, high-quality wine is produced in many regions of Greece. Several grape varieties, both traditionally Greek and foreign, flourish on the mainland or islands, producing exquisite red, rosé and white wines which, in recent years, have attracted the attention of wine lovers worldwide.

Retsina is a white wine produced exclusively in Greece using grape must treated with resin from the Aleppo pine.

It is the leftovers from the pressing of the grapes that are used to produce popular spirits like the anise-flavoured ouzo; tsipouro, which comes with or without anise; and raki, called tsikoudia in Crete. Anise-flavoured spirits have been popular in Greek-speaking areas since the time of the Byzantine Empire, when they were commonly served as an aperitif.

Since 2004, ouzo, tsipouro and raki have been recognized by the European Union as protected designation of origin products.

Finally, a traditional treat for guests is a home-made liqueur. Liqueurs are made in every region of Greece from produce that is locally available. Greece has liqueurs made of bitter cherries, oranges, mandarins, strawberries, cherries, berries and even chamomile! Internationally, Chios' masticha is the most renowned of Greek liqueurs.

---

*We should look for someone
to eat and drink with
before looking for something
to eat and drink.*

Epicurus
Greek philosopher
(341–270 BCE)